NO MORE
HOLES
IN MY
SHOES

NO MORE
HOLES
IN MY
SHOES

ANNA P. AMODEO

iUniverse, Inc.
Bloomington

No More Holes in My Shoes

iUniverse books may be ordered through booksellers or by contacting:

iUniverse
1663 Liberty Drive
Bloomington, IN 47403
www.iuniverse.com
1-800-Authors (1-800-288-4677)

ISBN: 978-1-4759-4463-1 (sc)
ISBN: 978-1-4759-4465-5 (hc)
ISBN: 978-1-4759-4464-8 (ebk)

Printed in the United States of America

iUniverse rev. date: 09/18/2012

I dedicate this book to my loving and caring husband,
Thomas J. Amodeo.

ACKNOWLEDGMENTS

I FIRST WANT TO THANK Our Lord and Blessed Mother, who got me to this beautiful spiritual life, for always being my guiding light. My gratitude also goes out to many others:

My prayerful, loving, and caring husband, Tom.

My dad, Michael Pascale, who went to his eternal home at the age of thirty-seven, leaving me at the age of fourteen months.

My mom, who sacrificed her life for her children and went to her eternal home at thirty-nine, leaving me at the age of eight years, an orphan.

My aunt Jennie and uncle Pete Carofano, who took care of me and my siblings after my mom's death.

My brothers Tony, Nunzi, and Meno and my sisters Mary and Millie, who always watched over me.

My granddaughter Maria Ronk, whose life ended tragically in a house fire when she was eleven years old.

Father Hanley of St. Mary's Church, who assisted my mom spiritually and monetarily.

Mary Lou Mahan, who gave me some advice on writing a book and has been very helpful.

John Tumminia, whom I encountered one morning after daily mass. His input, guidance, and interest in this project helped me.

Deacon Vinnie Porcelli, my son-in-law, and my daughter Donna, who spent the last month of Tom's life living with us. Vinnie made Tom very comfortable by bathing him, shaving him, and getting up at night when he needed attention. It was a great help to me. Tom enjoyed their company along with the many hours Kathy and Cindy spent with him. He was always happy when his family surrounded him.

Gerri Pascale Taddeo, my niece, who graciously helped me by putting the pages of this book together. She gave up some of her evenings and weekends. Thanks, Gerri, and God bless.

Julie Amodeo, who graciously accepted reading my book and who is an English major and was helpful in its writing.

Emily Amodeo, who assisted me in locating newspaper items in the library.

My lovely daughters, Kathy, Donna, and Cindy, and their spouses.

My grandchildren, Tommy Porcelli, Elizabeth Schaffer and Bob, Joelle and Brian Hannabery, and Matthew Schaffer and Amy.

My great-grandchildren—"the Schaffer girls," Morgan, Abbey, Emily, Katie, and Rebecca; Siena and Blake Hannaberry; and Beau and Haley Henry.

Preface

THIS IS THE STORY OF a woman who had every excuse to remain on the ground each time the World put her there, but rose up each time by simply reaching out to grab God's hand. It's the story of God's love and Poppy's love and the way that my Grandmother's faith in both never wavered. The truth is that in her love of our Father she knew God's word. "Through wisdom a house is built, and by understanding it is established; and by knowledge the rooms shall be filled with all precious and pleasant riches." Proverbs 24:3-4

So many of the experiences that appear in this memoir are matter of fact; some mouth-watering, some eye-watering, and some heart-breaking. These same experiences are those that took a lifetime of faith, forgiveness, and love to have the ability to even share.

This book and it's contents are a lifetime of memories, truths, and a testament to God's love. This is the story of Anna Pascale-Amodeo. This is the story of my Grandmother. This is the collection of truths that remind me tht God's love and Poppy's love is ever present.

EA Schaffer C

Introduction

I FOUND MYSELF SITTING ON my front porch in my favorite white wicker chair. The chair, like so many of my earthly belongings, has special meaning for me. My late husband, Tom, bought it for me as a gift, not for any special occasion, but just for the pleasure of seeing a smile on my face. Behind me was the front door to my home. Painted bright white, the door almost seemed to glow in spots as the summer sun leaked through the red maple tree on my front lawn and reflected off of it. The door serves as a background on which I display my beloved picture of the Lord. Something made me glance over my shoulder at the picture, and when I looked at the Lord's face, I felt a wave of peace resonate through my body.

It was at that moment that I realized I was going to be celebrating my eighty-fifth birthday in a few days. My mind started to drift away from my current surroundings, from the warmth of the beautiful sunny day, the sounds of the cars coming down the steep hill of Bloom Street, and the purring of lawnmowers as my neighbors busily worked on their yards. As the world remained busy around me, my mind wandered back as far as I could remember. I had endured times of darkness, sadness, and pain in my lifetime.

And I decided to write.

THE BEGINNINGS

My father was Michael Pascale. At five feet eleven inches, he was a very strong man, and he had a reputation for being reliable and hardworking. These qualities earned him respect from all of his friends. He was born in Monteforte, Italy, a small farming village whose rich soil was well known for producing sweet, juicy figs and hearty chestnuts. Like so many young men of his time, my father made the difficult decision to leave Italy and begin a new life in America. He agonized over this decision, as it would mean leaving behind his mom, dad, two sisters, and two brothers, and family meant so much to him.

My father had a friend named John Rizzo who was also from Monteforte. He had settled in Poughkeepsie, New York, a few years earlier. John and my father had kept in contact through occasional correspondence, and when my dad immigrated to the United States, he decided to settle in Poughkeepsie too since he knew John, and it would be comforting to have a connection from his hometown.

My mother, Mary Cioffi Pascale, was born in Naples, Italy, to a dress designer and police chief. My mom was very attractive. She wore a size eight dress and had a beautiful figure. Her complexion was flawless, and she had high, prominent cheekbones. She was educated and was able to read and write in Italian. In Italy, she had a position in her town's government as a secretary.

My mother's sister and brother-in-law, Jennie and Peter Carofano, had left for America while my mom was attending school and settled in Poughkeepsie too. My aunt Jennie was tall and had what we would now consider a full figure. She was a very kind and compassionate

1

woman. My uncle was a quite stocky man of average height, and there wasn't a kinder person than my uncle Pete Carofano.

One Sunday afternoon John asked my dad if he would like to meet his friends from Naples. They went over to the home of his friends Jennie and Peter Carofano, who warmly welcomed them. Jennie set out a plate of sliced sharp provolone cheese along with a glass of rich burgundy wine. Their conversation touched upon their family memories and the friends they had left behind in Italy. My aunt brought up the fact that she had a sister who was still living at home. She found a black-and-white photo that she kept of her and showed it to my dad. He was very impressed by the photo of my aunt Jennie's sister. He decided that he would write to her, and they corresponded for six months.

He had a little money put away and was able to send for her to come to America, where they could finally meet each other. She arrived at Ellis Island within three months. My dad anxiously awaited her arrival. He spotted her immediately in the great mass of people because she stood out in the crowd in her blue dress. My mom was rather shy, but they did greet each other with a hug. It was love at first sight.

My mom moved in with her sister Jennie and began working part-time in a clothing store, contributing some of her pay toward my aunt's household expenses. My aunt now had two daughters, Jennie and Katie, who kept her very busy. My father kept a small two-room apartment just two blocks away.

After courting for three months, my mom and dad decided to marry. They were wed in a Catholic church, with John and Ida Rizzo serving as their attendants. My aunt honored them with a modest reception at her home. It was a simple but very traditional gathering. There were rolls stuffed with prosciutto, salami, and imported cheese. Hearty bowls of large green and black olives and strips of eggplant soaked in olive oil, vinegar, and oregano lined the long food table. There were pitchers of beer and soda to drink. A beautiful wedding cake was displayed on a small wooden table in one corner of the room. It was a white cake with a rich cannoli filling and a sweet buttercream icing. Written in script across the top of the cake was "God Bless Mary and Michael."

My mom was asked to say a few words before the cutting of the cake. She did not like to be the center of attention, but she was so grateful for such a wonderful day that she stood by the cake and spoke without inhibition. She thanked my aunt and uncle for letting her stay there and for hosting such a joyous reception for her and her wonderful husband.

Her eyes began to tear as she thought of how she wished her mother and father could have been there to share in this beautiful day.

Italian records played throughout the reception. While the guests were served coffee and cake, my mom and dad danced to "Ti Voule Bena" ("I Love You"). Their smiles radiated the happiness and love they felt for each other. They were anxious to start their lives together as husband and wife. Oh, what dreams and expectations they had.

Their friends finished the evening with the delicious cake, and everyone took home a small box of almond candies as a favor.

About a month after the wedding, Ida and John Rizzo and their sons moved to Hoboken, New Jersey. Mr. Rizzo had success in finding work in a shirt factory in Hoboken and offered my dad a position in the factory, so six months later, my parents followed them there. Mr. Rizzo helped my parents to find an apartment. He was such a dear friend to my dad; he treated him as if they were brothers. My dad worked in the shirt factory during the week and as a bartender on the weekends. My aunt Jennie missed her sister when she moved to Hoboken but realized that things would be better for her.

It was in Hoboken that their first child was born, a son. He was named after our grandfather, Antonio Pasquale, but the name was Americanized to Anthony (Tony) Pascale. After three years in Hoboken, my dad was offered a job as a foreman in a clothing factory in West New York, New Jersey. His experience in the shirt factory had opened the door to a higher position. He and my mom moved into a larger apartment, and Tony had his own room, which was a luxury at that time. It was in West New York that their second child was born. This time it was a daughter, whom they named Mary. A year and a half after Mary was born, their third child, Nunzio (John), came into the world, and two years later, in 1921, Carmen (Meno) was born.

Michael Pascale

Mary Pascale

Our First Home

MY DAD HAD ALWAYS YEARNED to live in the country and perhaps have a small farm of his own. After 3 years he decided to check with Aunt Jennie and Uncle Pete to see if they knew of any land for sale in the Poughkeepsie area. They informed him that there was a small farm with a house for sale in Marlboro, New York, across the Hudson River from Poughkeepsie..

In the meantime my aunt and uncle had purchased ten acres of farmland in Marlboro from a man named Mr. Brown. The property was located in the center of the village and was adjacent to Mr. Brown's property. They built a large farmhouse with four apartments in it. Mr. Brown held the mortgage on the ten acres, and they would pay Mr. Brown twice a year, in January and June, in the amount of $120 for the interest. They had saved enough money to pay the contractor a substantial down payment for the farmhouse, and they borrowed the rest of the money to build it from the First National Bank of Marlboro. They purchased building supplies at Abbey's Lumber Co. in Newburgh and VanVliet's block company and used Sam Filligram's dad for their contractor. After the house was completed, they lived in one and and three apartments quickly rented. (This house was torn down in 1999 to construct a senior citizen housing complex called Jennie's Garden, named after my aunt.)

Expanding the farm to increase fruit production was very laborious. The family spent many long, hard hours planting more strawberry plants, currants, gooseberries, and different fruit trees. The soil had to be worked in order to produce fruit of good quality.

My uncle worked at the stone crusher plant during the week and then worked all weekend on the farm. My aunt hired a man named Dominick to help with the chores. Dominick was a very sweet man with the most beautiful blue eyes. His wages consisted of very little money, but in return for his labor he was furnished with meals and a place to sleep in the small barn. With the little bit of money that he earned, he would buy tobacco for his pipe and a pint of wine for fifteen cents. He did not work on Sunday, so that was the day he could be found on the concrete porch of the big house enjoying the wine. The wine was homemade from the concord grapes that my aunt had on the farm. Every September the concord grapes were ready to be harvested and pressed to produce the wine. My uncle would usually make a barrel for their own use.

My mom and dad were still considering the move to Marlboro. Mr. Rizzo drove them up to see a little farm and house located on South Road, and they made the decision to move away from the apartment in the city to a home of their own in the country on this quaint little farm.

My dad gave notice to the owner of the factory where he was employed and thanked him for the modest salary that he had received. He had saved enough to put a down payment on the farm, and for the rest, my dad went to the First National Bank of Marlboro for a loan. He was granted the loan, and my parents' dreams of being landowners got under way.

Owning their first home was such a proud moment for them. All of their previous living quarters had been apartments. The house was almost square in shape and had two floors. There was an enclosed porch on the front of the house, which sat close to a dirt road. In the back of the house there was land, which my dad cleared to plant more fruit plants such as strawberries, currants, and raspberries. In the spring he would plant rows of tomatoes, and after they were picked, my dad would help my mom carry the full bushels of tomatoes into the kitchen. Some of the tomatoes, they canned for the winter season. My mom would start the canning process early in the morning and not stop until noon. She always labored for about a week straight. The fresh basil she added was so green against the red of the fresh tomatoes.

Some of our neighbors were the Alonges, Troncillitos, and Affusos. They were very kind people.

Our first house

OUR FIRST HOUSE

One of the first things that my parents did was enroll Tony, Mary, and John in school; they would attend the one on Lattintown Road. My father then invested in a horse and buggy. It was convenient to buy groceries in town at Fred Fowler's store and food for the horse and chickens that were now a part of our farm at Baxter's feed store. The family enjoyed the fresh eggs. Yes, my dad was quite happy with his new lifestyle and his little farm.

The kids walked to school, and it was quite a long trek for them. My mom started to make her own jam from the concord grapes harvested on the farm. For the kids' school lunches, she would prepare a sandwich of peanut butter from the village store and her jam and wrap it in wax paper and add a piece of whatever fruit was in season, all placed in a small brown paper bag.

The first year on the farm was very prosperous. The harvested fruit had yielded a good profit, and my parents were able to pay not just the interest on the loan but two thousand dollars on the principal. Things were finally looking up in their new venture. Finally, my sister Millie was added to the family, and eighteen months later, I came along.

My mom and dad were so happy with the way their lives were going, and they decided to invite Mr. and Mrs. Rizzo and their two sons for a long weekend. My mom started to plan the dinners that she would prepare. She wanted to make sure she had all the ingredients for homemade bread and pasta and a rich tomato sauce with meatballs and sausage.

The morning before they arrived Dad got on his horse and buggy and traveled down South Road to Western Avenue to Fred Fowler's store for flour, yeast, garlic, onions, and a vanilla loaf cake. He then stopped at Kniffen's meat market for the chop meat, sausage, and a piece of center cut pork loin for the tomato sauce. He hurried home to get the meat in the icebox. The icebox sure looked good when it was stocked.

Everyone was excited that we were going to have company. Now we had to plan how we were going to sleep. My aunt had an extra mattress, which my dad borrowed. My brothers, Tony and John, went with him to cart it home. They really enjoyed riding with the horse and buggy and spending time with Dad. It was decided that my brothers would sleep on the mattress, Mr. and Mrs. Rizzo would use my brothers' bed, and their sons would sleep on another mattress we had.

The Rizzos arrived near noontime. They had bags of groceries, including Italian cold cuts, cheese, olives, a big white box full of Italian pastries, and two quarts of red wine. As soon as the guests were settled, everyone gathered around the kitchen table, where the delicious Italian cold cuts of prosciutto, salami, and cheese had been set out on a beautiful platter. Sliced tomatoes and black and green olives were served on another matching dish. My mom's homemade bread was arranged in a silver bread dish, which was one of her most cherished wedding gifts. Wine was served in my mom's special crystal glasses, another wedding gift. There was soda for the children, which was a special treat. The meal was followed with the luscious pastries. What a beautiful lunch.

After lunch the adults gathered on the screened porch. A warm June breeze set just the right atmosphere, and they sipped their demitasse flavored with anisette as they remembered old friends from Monteforte.

My brothers and the Rizzo boys walked down South Road to the Lattintown schoolhouse. They could not believe how small the school was—it was just a one-room building. When they returned, they joined the adults, who were still gathered on the porch.

That evening's dinner was a late meal because lunch had been so large and filling. As the group prepared for the meal, the lasagna was in the oven at 350, and the sauce was warming. Mom had made the salad that morning. She always liked a hearty salad. She would mix different greens such as romaine, iceberg, and green leaf lettuce and add red onion, celery, tomato, and black olives. She would then season the salad with just the right amount of salt, pepper, olive oil, and red vinegar, to which she added a clove of garlic to make it more flavorful.

The kitchen table was now set for a group of twelve. My mom took the lasagna out of the oven and placed the pan on the counter near the stove. She cut the lasagna in perfect squares, and the ricotta and the mozzarella cheese stood firmly under the pasta. Each serving was covered with the sauce, and my sister Mary placed each dish at the table. The rich grated cheese was served in two small dishes placed at each end of the table. There was also red crushed pepper and black pepper.

My father stood at the head of the table and said the blessing in Italian. He thanked the Lord for all the blessings bestowed upon our family and for the presence of his sincere friends, the Rizzo family. It was quiet after the blessing because no one could wait to share this wonderful meal. My father proudly served the first wine that he had harvested from his concord grapes.

The following morning, the Rizzos departed for their home in Hoboken. They thanked my parents for the wonderful visit.

With fall approaching, my dad became very busy with trimming the fruit trees as well as the grape vines. It also would soon be time for the older children to return to school, which meant new school clothes. My mom took the boys for their clothes in Newburgh one day and took Mary another day. Mr. Troncillito, a neighbor, would drive his wife and my mom to Newburgh to J.C. Penney, which we called Penney's. They were able to purchase their clothes and shoes in the same store, which was very convenient. My brothers and sister were always excited for the first day of school. They loved wearing their new clothes and shoes.

My parents did all their grocery shopping at Fred Fowler's store, which was known as the "Snowball Store." "Snowball" was the brand name of canned goods that he carried in the store. The store was one large, long room with a small room in the back that was used for storage. The shelves were packed to the fullest. Large brown boxes usually sat on the floor as the storage room was filled to capacity. A large awning went across the length of the store. Under the awning all kinds of fresh vegetables could be found. A large bunch of bananas could always be found at one end of the display, and at the other end hung a large silver scale. There were stiff brown paper bags on hand in which the produce could be put. Inside the store was a large icebox containing butter and milk.

Our meat products were bought at Kniffen's Meat Market, which was located on the left side of the post office. It was a very small store. There was a small counter covered with a thick wooden block. The meat was cut in front of you after you ordered. There was no prepackaging. There was a very small refrigerator room where the meat was stored. I remember my mother saying that the butcher, Jim, was always so pleasant.

One spring morning, everyone was going about the typical routine. The older children headed off to school, and later that morning my mom put me in my crib for a morning nap. My mom and dad went outside with Millie and Meno to clean some brush that was left from the fall. While they were out doing these chores, the house caught on fire, but they were not able to see the house from where they were working, down over a small bank.

Charlie Pedrone, a young man in his twenties from out of town, was out taking his morning walk. He was in town visiting his relatives, the Affuso family. He heard some voices, which he thought was quite unusual for that time of day since the children were in school. He turned to where the voices were coming from and saw flames. He ran toward the burning house. Bystanders were screaming that there was a baby in the house. Against their advice, he entered the burning structure, hoping that he would be able to find the baby. He came out of the house with me wrapped in his white T-shirt, which he had used to shield me from the overpowering smoke.

I was told that he was unable to speak at first. The people there could see the fright in his eyes, and the sweat just ran down his face, streaking through the black soot that tinged his skin. The darkness and the smoke were so intense that he hadn't thought he would make it out alive. He knew that it was a race against time and that every second that he searched for me was important. He felt as if his body was flying from the burning house. He told the people outside the house that he'd had to follow the sound of my cries to get to me because he was not familiar with the layout of the house.

Meanwhile, my parents started back to the house. They could hear commotion but had no idea what it was until they saw their home going up in flames. The flames were now more intense and had fully engulfed the house.

My parents thought that I was still in the house and had no idea that Charles Pedrone, the hero, had risked his life to rescue me. Overcome by grief, my mother fainted in the arms of one of the neighbors. They hurried to tell her that I was safe and that one of the other neighbors had taken me to her home to clean me up and comfort me.

My dad was in shock but was very thankful to Charles Pedrone for putting his life on the line to save mine. He did remember lighting the coal stove that morning to get the chill out of the house. Some dish towels had been left on the chair near the stove to dry, and apparently, they had ignited in flames.

My parents were thankful that I was saved. Now they had to gather their composure to see where they would go from here. They were devastated, as were the children when they arrived home from school to hear the news about our home.

My parents then had the task of rebuilding their home. This took quite a toll on their financial situation.

In the late 1980s I received a phone call from Camille Affuso, telling me that there was a man at her house who wanted to meet me. I couldn't imagine who it could be, so I dressed up and went to Camille's house. As I parked the car and walked up the sidewalk toward the house, I noticed an elderly man sitting on the screened-in porch. As I entered, Camille said, "Anne, this is my uncle, Charles Pedrone, who saved you in the house fire." I gave him a big hug and thanked him profusely.

He was overcome with joy to see me. With a big smile on his face, he jokingly said, "Let me see if I can pick you up now." He was living in New York City and was retired but had been in the jewelry business.

It was a big surprise for me to meet this fine gentleman who had saved my life. I spent an hour with Camille and her uncle Charles. We talked about the many different times that he had visited Marlboro.

Bottom row (l-r): Tony Pascale, Thomas Amodeo, Anne Pascale Amodeo, Mary (Falco) Rosamelia
Top row (l-r): Carmen Pascale, Fannie Pascale, Margaret Deciano Hager, Daisy Pascale, John Pascale, Millie Sadler, Robert Sadler, Sal Rosamelia

The First Tragedy

<hr>

As I mentioned before, my dad was a very strong man. But after the fire his health began to go downhill. He lost his appetite and struggled with his breathing. When he went to the local doctor, Dr. Harris told him it was probably from the fright of the fire. The doctor tried different medications but to no avail. His health was quickly deteriorating, and he was unable to do his farm work. The Troncillitos and the Affusos, our neighbors, pitched in to help out on the farm.

One morning my mother decided that my dad should see a specialist in New York. Dr. Harris gave her the name of an outstanding doctor and made an appointment for my dad. He gave the specialist some history of my father's health. Mr. James Festa, a family friend, was always there to help, and he drove my mom and dad to New York City. After a thorough examination, the doctor said that he couldn't find anything wrong.

My father constantly complained about his breathing. There were no x-rays back in 1926, which would have been helpful to evaluate his lungs. He was given some pills to take that were supposed to relax him. But there was still no improvement in his breathing. Could it have been lung cancer? His three sons later in life passed on because of lung cancer. You did not hear too much about lung cancer in those days.

One morning my dad was just not doing well at all. He was struggling with each breath that he took. My mom decided to call Dr. Zachary, a new physician in town. He came to the house with his black medical bag and checked him out. After hearing all my dad's medical history, he decided it could very well be his tonsils. On the small table in the living room he placed his tools to prepare for the procedure.

13

After this procedure was done, my father lay on the couch and slowly bled to death at the age of thirty-seven. His death certificate recorded peritonsilar abcess as the cause of death.

My uncle Pete and aunt Jennie were present, as were the Troncillitos and a nun from St. Cabrini's Orphanage in West Park. The children were all present too, but I was an infant. The older siblings, Mary and Tony, remember the horrible sight of seeing their father, who they loved so much, in agony, slowly bleeding to death in front of their eyes. What a devastating experience for the whole family to witness. My dad was laid out in the house that he loved. He passed away on September 22, 1926.

In those days friends and family would donate money for the funeral expenses. A book was usually kept with the names and the amount of money given. With these donations my mother was able to pay for the funeral. Father Hanley, the priest from St. Mary's Church, gave a beautiful eulogy. My mom had a strong faith and would confide her worries to him. My dad was buried in St. Mary's Cemetery in Marlborough.

My mom was now left with six children and a mortgage to pay. She was so devastated over losing the man she loved so much. Her dream was falling apart, but she had to stay strong for the children. It wasn't long before she fell behind in her mortgage payments, land and school taxes, and utility bills. Unable to make the payments, she lost the house and the farm that both she and her husband had loved.

To this day whenever I pass the house, a feeling of sadness encompasses me. I think of what my parents went through after the house fire and my dad's tragic death in the house.

My aunt Jennie and uncle Pete were living on the property near Western Avenue that they had purchased from Mr. Brown, in the house that had the four apartments on the third floor. There were two apartments on each floor that were made of four rooms in a row. They used to call them "railroad apartments" because the rooms lined up one after the other. Our family moved into one of the apartments. The hallway was narrow and dark, and one lone light bulb hanging down on a wire was used to light the long dark hallway. It created a very eerie atmosphere in the hall. You would find yourself running through the halls just out of fear of the darkness.

The apartment was heated with a coal stove. The coal was delivered by Mazzola Trucking Company in Newburgh into a small window in the cellar, and each tenant had a space where their coal was shoveled in.

I can remember my brothers, Tony and John, taking turns filling a large metal pail with our share of coal from the cellar. They would each take a handle of the pail and carry it up the narrow stairway to our apartment. This was our main source of heat and how we kept our living quarters warm. The large black stove was located in middle of our kitchen, and a large pot of water was always kept hot on the stove. We would use this for hot water and for washing the dishes.

During the real cold months, we used a small kerosene stove in the end bedroom, with the door kept open to the other bedrooms, so that the small amount of heat would pass through and spread. There was just one toilet in the cold hallway, which we shared with the other apartment across from ours. There was always a waiting line, but it wasn't long before each tenant had their own bathroom. Shortly after we moved in, the bathrooms were updated. Many other improvements were made. In our kitchen we had a small icebox installed, and Jessie Elliott, a Marlboro iceman, would deliver small blocks of ice. We kept our milk, butter, and small amounts of meat in it. In the winter we had a small wooden box outside our kitchen window, nailed to the frame of the window. It was sufficient to keep our dairy products fresh. As the weather got warmer, the box would be taken in and saved for the following year, and the icebox would then be used.

At the end of my aunt and uncle's property was a brook. Mr. Festa, a neighbor and family friend, gave my aunt and uncle the right of way down his driveway. A small bridge was built over the brook that gave us access to Western Ave, which was the main street in town. We were able to go to the grocery store, post office, St. Mary's Church, and other businesses. Without the bridge or Mr. Festa's driveway, cars and trucks would be unable to get to the farmhouse, so Mr. Festa's gesture was very kind. In addition to this kind act, he was always there to help in any emergency, and his car was always ready if we needed a ride somewhere. We didn't have a phone, but Mrs. Festa, or Nettie, as we called her, always relayed any important messages such as a doctor's call or the death of one of our distant relatives.

On the east side of the property was a cold running spring. We really enjoyed this spring in the summer. On the right side of the property was a gray barn converted from an ice barn. The bottom floor of the barn housed a horse who was used to pull the plow and pull the cart loaded with fresh picked fruit. The fruit then would be stored on the front porch until it was picked up by a truck, which would then deliver it to New York City where it would be sold.

We were getting adjusted in our apartment. But it was the beginning of a bad year. With the cost of coal to heat the four-room apartment, electricity, rent, and the cost of food, not to mention clothing and shoes, my mother found herself in enormous debt. She did get some help from the county; however, it still was very difficult to make ends meet.

My brother Tony had taken on the role of a father figure since he was the oldest son. He dropped out of school and got a job with Joe DallVechia's Trucking. He was a hard worker and was very determined to keep the family together. The DallVechias were very kind to him and to our family. I remember Julia DallVechia coming with her son, Jigger, with groceries and fruit baskets during the holidays.

In today's world my mom would have been able to receive food stamps and Medicaid. She also would have been eligible to have her rent and fuel paid for. My brother Tony would have been able to continue with his education.

In the summer we would pick berries on my aunt's farm, and the money that we earned was deducted from our rent. When my aunt's berries were all picked, we would travel to other fruit farms to find work picking berries. I hated having to work in the scalding hot sun. There was no way to get away from it because the berries were in fields that had no trees for shade. Trying to fill a quart with these small berries was a very tedious job. I promised myself that I would never marry a farmer. However, for now I had no choice, so I continued picking berries the rest of the summer.

One farm where Millie, Carmen, and I went to pick berries was the DallVechia farm, on Plattekill Road. Betty DallVechia, one of the daughters, was in charge of counting the quarts that were picked. She was always dressed so cute, and she was able to stay in the shade of the cool barn. I always wished that I had her job.

We picked at least fifty quarts each and were paid two and a half cents per quart. The money that we earned went toward our school clothes. At the end of the picking season we still hadn't earned enough money for our clothes and shoes. Mr. Festa brought my mom to social services to see if she could get more assistance for our family. She was able to get permission for our shoes to be supplied by the county.

In order for us to get our shoes, we had to get approval from the Poor Master. He lived on 9W, directly opposite of the Sunoco Station. He was a short, fat, and very grumpy man with a face the shape of a large round ball. His complexion was a bright cherry red. After our first encounter with him we were petrified to go back.

When we did have to make a visit to update our shoes, my sister Millie and I would gather all our courage before we approached his front door. There was a long narrow window on the left side of the door. My sister would ring the bell, and then we would jump to the side because we were frightened at the sight of him peering through the window. He would throw open the door and glare at us with his angry red face. At the sight of him, our bodies would immediately stiffen up. It was like our feet were frozen to his old wooden porch. My sister always did the talking, and she let him know that we were there because we needed to get a new pair of shoes.

He would then clench his teeth on his curly stemmed pipe and glare down at us. His reply was always the same. He would raise his voice and say, "You just got a new pair." It was after he belittled us that we would pick up our feet and show him the holes in the bottom of our tattered shoes.

Then he would agree that we were in need of new shoes and would proceed to fill out the request form for us. We were always so relieved when he finally handed us the permission slip that we would take it from his grubby hands and practically run from his old wooden porch. We would then take the slip to Herbrech's Variety Store, in the center of Marlboro, on Western Avenue (now Dr. Schencker's office).

Boy, how we dreaded going to the Poor Master for shoes. It is now seventy-six years later, and I shall never, for as long as I live, forget his angry red face with his curly stemmed pipe sticking out of the corner of his mouth.

Besides having to beg for shoes, I was made fun of by one of my classmates. (Our school building was on Western Avenue, where today's American Legion Hall stands. Prior to being a classroom, it was a button sorting factory. There were always buttons to be found on the ground outside of the building. Some were whole, and many were just broken pieces. They were there for many years.) I wore mostly ill-fitting hand-me-down clothes that were too big or too long. This classmate always referred to me as "grandma." I never said a word back to him, but I could feel the tears welling up in my eyes whenever we had a confrontation. I never told my mom about it, as she was always sick and worried about where the next penny would come from for food and other necessities, and I didn't want to add to her worries. Eddie always had a silly grin on his face, which was just full of freckles. We sat in the back of the class, so our teacher, Mrs. Lowery, was not aware of what was going on.

The classmate moved some years later to the town of Newburgh and graduated from the Newburgh schools. I got closure when we had our ten-year class reunion in 1954 Marlboro, and I was on the committee to contact our former classmates. I went one step further and looked up this former classmate and added him to the invitation list. Even though he hadn't graduated with our class, the committee thought the former students would like to see him because he had been known as the class clown. I was sure happy, as I wanted to get even with him. I was very pleased when he responded that he and his wife would be attending the reunion.

When my husband Tom (I was married by then) and I entered the cocktail room at the Holiday Inn in Newburgh, the first thing I did was ask Rose Diorio Minadeo, who was sitting at a small table checking in the attendees, "Is *he* here yet?" She directed me toward a table in the corner of the room. Well, to my surprise there stood a good-looking, well-polished man. I didn't waste any time heading right over to his table. I walked very proudly with my arm looped through the arm of my very handsome husband. I had waited so long for this moment. I was wearing a beautiful black form-fitting gown, a pearl necklace with matching earrings, and a bracelet. My look was completed with high-heel silver sandals. I wore my hair in an upsweep with a beautiful frosting, which was the current style for that time period.

He was sitting there with his wife. As Tom and I approached his table, he stood up and greeted us. I realized that he wasn't sure who I was. I spoke up and said, "Do you know who I am?"

He was silent for a second, and then he said, "Is this Anna Pascale?" He commented on how beautiful I looked.

With much pride, I introduced him to my husband. I was so proud of my husband, who looked exceptionally handsome that night. He was dressed in an off-white suit, black shirt, and matching tie. Then right away I said to the man, "Do you remember calling me 'grandma' in grade school?" He apologized and again said how beautiful I looked.

I felt I got some closure, but the hurt from the teasing never really left me completely. I don't think this classmate realized the humiliation and pain that he caused me. I was a young girl who did not have all the advantages that the other students had, and his name-calling hurt me deeply.

During the course of the evening, we discussed our lives. He was working with Metro Life Insurance and was going to be transferred to Ohio. I was very happy that the committee had decided to invite him and his wife and that I had had the chance to confront him after all those years.

I disliked school not just because of being called "grandma" but also because most of the students would bring in some storybooks from home. These were books that their parents had bought and would read to them. My mom could not afford to buy any storybooks. For that matter she did not know how to read in English. This always made me feel like the other students were superior to me.

I started to feel better about myself in the fourth and fifth grades. Miss Dowd was my fourth grade teacher. She was very kind and always praised me and gave me a lot of confidence. It was such a beautiful feeling to be part of the class. Miss Bewick was my fifth grade teacher and was familiar with my home life. She continued to give the attention and confidence that Miss Dowd had given me.

As for my sixth grade teacher, I do not have the same good memories. I must say she was one of the teachers who had pets, and I was not one of them. In later years she was very pleasant to me. I always wanted to be a better student and would stay after school for extra help, and that sure did help as I got into the higher grades.

Things at home were not getting any better financially. The assistance from the county and the money that my brother Tony earned working just did not add up to enough income. My brother John quit school and started to learn the barber trade. He became the barber for Tony's Barber Shop on 9W next to the Raccoon Saloon.

Fred Fowler was kind enough to give my mom credit at his store and wait for a weekly payment. One day Mr. Festa took my mom to the county office in Kingston to see if she could get more assistance, to help us get by. Mrs. Malfa, a friend, stayed with my sister and me. I remember that the icebox had only a half-quart of milk, an almost empty jar of jelly, and a peanut butter jar with only an inch of peanut butter left at the bottom. In the bread box on the counter was a half-loaf of stale bread.

We were anxious for our mother to come home so we could find out if she got any more assistance. Finally, we heard Mr. Festa's car pull into in the driveway, the car door close, and our mother come up the stairs and down the short hallway. As the kitchen door opened, we could tell by the expression on her face that it was bad news. Her face was tired and pale. We sat around the table to hear the news, and at that moment my three brothers walked in and joined us.

My mom sat there with tears streaming down her cheeks and proceeded with a very heavy heart to tell us about the outcome of her visit. The woman who interviewed her had said that she was receiving the maximum amount of assistance that she was entitled to. She had suggested that the only answer was to put Millie and me in an orphanage at St. Cabrini's in West Park, and our brother Carmen could go into a foster home. Mary could stay at home to help my mom and get some part-time work babysitting. My two older brothers had employment.

My mom was devastated to think that part of her family would be taken away. She would never consider such an option. This news was very upsetting to us children. The thought of being taken from our mother and family was just horrible. My mother cried constantly. She was just so distraught.

Aunt Jennie and Uncle Pete's Farm House

My Mother's Life-Changing Decision

ONE DAY A FRIEND OF my mother told her about a single, hardworking man who lived in Newburgh. His name was Phillip Deciano. This friend thought he would make a good husband and be a good provider. Marriage was the furthest thing from my mother's mind, though. She'd had shared a true love with my father and was still devoted to him.

Finally there came a point when my mother had no choice but to marry this man. She agreed to marry Phillip, as she saw no other way to keep her family together and to get us out of debt. It was a desperate move for her. The ceremony was very quiet. There was no party or celebration. My mom sacrificed her life for us the day she married him. Her life and ours would never be the same.

Phillip was of average height and small framed. He was a good-looking man; his features included deep brown eyes and very dark curly hair. He was a good provider, but his downside was that he was also very controlling.

I was only fourteen months old when my dad died, so I didn't remember him at all. I grew up in my early years thinking that Phillip was my biological father. It didn't take long to learn otherwise. We were very frightened of him. We were afraid to even speak around him because we felt if we said the wrong thing, we would get slapped across the face.

My mom and Phillip had two children together, Margaret and Joey. They were beautiful children who resembled their father with their dark hair and eyes. I loved them dearly.

There was one incident with Phillip that I don't remember because I was too young, but I have a scar over my left eye to prove it happened. My mom and Phillip and I were walking to the bus stop where Key Bank is located now on Route 9W. My mom had to go to Newburgh to Burger's Furniture to buy a new mattress for my brother's bed. Because he thought I wasn't walking fast enough, Phillip pushed me, and I fell, which resulted in a gash over my left eye. This was very upsetting for my mom.

I remember another incident very clearly, as I was six-and-a-half years old. It was a beautiful sunny afternoon. My sisters Millie and Margaret and I went to get ice cream cones. Mrs. Coutant had a small ice cream store in her house on Western Avenue, just past the Legion Hall. She would make a huge ice cream cone for five cents. After we bought the ice cream cones, we decided to go home via Birdsall Avenue rather than the way we came, via Western Avenue, which would take us ten minutes longer. In order to get to the farmhouse, we had to go through Mr. Brown's farm because there was no road in from Birdsall Avenue. As we were walking through the rows of grapes to get home, we heard someone behind us. We turned to see Phillip standing there holding a shotgun. We started to run as fast as we could around the grape patch. When I looked around, I saw that he had run down the row where Millie was running. I must say I was somewhat relieved that he had gone down her row and not mine. I heard one of the neighbors yell at Phillip to stop. Thank God he did. Phillip was very angry because it had taken us those ten minutes longer to get home, and Millie got the blame because she was the oldest of the three of us.

My mom heard the commotion and came downstairs. Guns were nothing to him. He always slept with a gun at his side. But she was unaware that he had gone after us. She wanted to contact the authorities to report his abusiveness. But she was talked out of it by her friends. They told her to give him another chance.

One thing that I remember and that always stayed in my mind was Phillip reading this large book written in Italian. It was a very fine print. At the top of one of the pages there was a platter with a human head on it. Until this day I don't know if it was the Bible, an Italian fiction story, or a Mafia story.

Even though friends talked my mom out of calling the authorities, she did speak to Mr. John Rusk, a lawyer in town, about the incident. He said there wasn't much to be done unless an act happened.

Phillip and my brother Tony did not get along too well. Tony did not like the way that Phillip treated my mother and the rest of the family. Phillip saw Tony as an adversary because he had now grown into a young man and was a physical threat to him. Philip found fault with everything my mom did as well as what any of us children did.

He had very strict rules, and we had to abide by them. I remember we all had to sit down at the same time for our dinner. He demanded that we eat in silence, and there was to be no discussion of any kind at the dinner table. If any of us did not like what was prepared for dinner, then we had to leave the table and go to our room until the others were done with their meal.

I remember one night we were having rice and beans for dinner, and my cousin Rocky, who lived downstairs, came upstairs to visit. Phillip asked him if he would like to have a dish of rice and beans, and Rocky said no. Phillip immediately told him to get downstairs.

Another incident was with my brother Carmen. He had forgotten to feed Phillip's rabbits when he got home from school. That day my mom was sick in bed, as her health was now starting to fail. She heard Phillip hollering at Carmen, and she knew he would be slapped around. She got out of bed and stood on the upper porch of the farmhouse. She was so frail and thin, and her face was so pale. She called out for Phillip to stop beating Carmen.

On Ash Wednesday my brother John, Carmen, Mary, Millie, and I went to St. Mary's Church for service, and the service ran longer than usual. Father Hanley gave a very long homily. When we got home, Phillip was waiting for us with his belt in his hands. My brother John was the victim that night. Phillip waited until John got in bed, and then he went in and beat him with his belt. It was a trauma for my mom and us children.

My mom's health was really starting to worsen. She was always so sick. She was so pale and had lost so much weight that her skin just seemed to hang on her frame. My sister Mary would do the cooking and laundry, and Millie and I would do the cleaning. My mom always had that worried look on her face and was always so sad. Her worst fear was that if something happened to her, we would be left to deal with Phillip.

My mother went to see Dr. Ferguson, whose office was on Church Street. He recommended that she go to the clinic in Kingston. My mother was hemorrhaging and had to go to the clinic for treatments. Mr. Festa took her weekly, but her condition wasn't getting better, and the doctor from the clinic said that she would need surgery. Plans were made with a doctor from Newburgh for surgery to be done at St. Luke's.

I remember that my teacher, Mrs. Schaffer, was giving my class a spelling test when the classroom door opened. Everything was very quiet. My sister Mary came in and was greeted by Mrs. Schaffer. As they spoke to each other, I could tell something was very wrong from the expression on the teacher's face. Mary was there to get me, so that I could go home to say good-bye to my mom. Mr. Festa was taking her to the hospital. The surgeon had had a cancellation, and she was going in that day rather than two days later as planned.

As my sister Mary and I walked home from the school, a terrible thought came to my mind: *will my mom be okay?* I started to tremble at the thought of being left with Phillip if my mom's surgery should go wrong. My stomach was just sick with fear over what was happening with my mother. The short walk from the school seemed to take forever.

As I walked down Mrs. Festa's driveway, I noticed that the beautiful flowers she had planted on either side of her driveway were in bloom. Cars were traveling up and down Western Avenue, and the people walking in the village were happy. I could hear them laughing and carrying on conversation. How could life around me continue on when my world was crashing down around me? It seemed like the whole world should be sad.

From the bridge I could see Mr. Festa's car parked in front of the farmhouse. As I got up to the car, I saw my mom propped up in the backseat; she barely had enough strength to sit up. I could see the grief on her face. It was an image that I will never forget. She hugged and kissed me with tears running down her cheeks. I quickly ran inside so that she wouldn't see or hear my sobbing.

I feared that this was the last time I would see my mom alive. The memory I have of my mom that day was of a very frail woman. Her salt-and-pepper hair was pulled back in a bun at the base of her neck. She had a very worried look on her face, and tears were streaming down her cheeks.

As I relive that day, I too have tears running down my cheeks.

THROUGH FAITH WE SURVIVE

My mom had surgery the next day and needed three blood transfusions. As the blood was being administered, my uncle Pete noticed a change in my mom's body. He immediately called the nurse. In a moment my mom's bed was surrounded by nurses and the doctor on duty. My mom had a rare type of blood, and after checking her record, they noticed the wrong type of blood had been administered.

My uncle Pete was holding her head in his arms when she uttered, "Please take care of my children." He gave her a kiss on the cheek, and she closed her eyes forever.

We were all waiting at home to see how my mom made out with her surgery. The hospital was to call Mr. Festa's number to relay any messages. Mrs. Festa was the one to receive the terrible news. We saw her coming down the drive toward the house. We were hoping to hear that the surgery had gone well. But when she got closer to us, we could see that her eyes were red and swollen. She had been a very good friend to my mother. We now knew that the news was not good.

She tried to give us the news as gently as possible. She told us that Mom had gone home with the Lord. When I heard the news, the beautiful blue sky immediately became dark; the soft breeze from the fruit trees came to a halt. Cars were going up and down Western Avenue, but I couldn't hear them. At that moment my world came to an end.

Finally, reality set in, and we all began sobbing. I remember that my brother John was hysterical. Even though he was a son, he had taken on the role of my mother's caregiver. He always made sure that she took her medications and made her eggnog, to which he always added Ovaltine to give it a good flavor. My brother Carmen was trying to comfort John. Mary, Millie, and I just hugged each other and cried our hearts out. My brother Tony was at work. James Festa contacted Joe DallVechia to ask him to break the news of our mother's death to Tony. He came home immediately. He put up a strong front for us younger children, but his heart was also broken. He knew that there was much work ahead now that my mother was gone, and Phillip would want to take over the family. Phillip was not home at the time. He was visiting a friend and had taken his two children, Margaret and Joseph, with him. When he came home, he didn't have much of a reaction.

That morning my aunt Jennie had lit a candle in front of the Lady's statue. She had then gone to a small hill at the end of the farm to sit and pray in silence. Whenever she had a problem of any kind, she would go up the hill and sit on a large rock. She could see the farmhouse from this spot. When she saw us children and a few of the close neighbors gathered outside, she realized that it had to be very bad news. She quickly came down from her spot on the hill and over to the farmhouse. She wasn't able to walk too fast, as she had some problems with her legs and had to wear elastic stockings every day for some relief. When she got to the house, she hugged each one of us. She was sobbing so hard. She spoke in Italian as she expressed her grief over the loss of her sister, Mary. She was much too young to die, she said. Yes, thirty-nine years old was much too young.

Funeral arrangements were made with the Tuthill Funeral Home in Marlboro. My uncle, the Festas, Joe DallVechia, and neighbors all donated toward the funeral expenses. The morning of the viewing, Tuthill's hearse was parked in front of the farmhouse. It had delivered my mother's body back to our home. My mother's bedroom was cleared out, and the casket was placed in the room. I remember the casket was brown and lined with an off-white silky material. The flowers that had been placed in the room emitted an odd floral fragrance.

At first, we were hesitant about going into the room where her body was laid out. But we came to terms with the fact that it was our mother, and we needed to be with her. The first time I saw her lying there, I ran out of the room and to the cold porcelain toilet bowl, where I immediately emptied the contents of my stomach. Seeing her lying there confirmed that she was in fact gone, and I would never have her back again.

My mother's dress was a light blue. Her friend Mrs. Malfa had bought it at Sterns in Poughkeepsie. Her hair was combed lightly in a soft bun. She looked like she was asleep, too young but at last at peace.

The day of the funeral, Julia DallVechia picked me up early in the morning. She was going to dress me up for the day. She dressed me in a beautiful pink organdy dress, white shoes, and pink socks and placed a pink bow in my fine straight hair. For the first time in my life, I felt like a princess. This situation was pretty ironic. I wondered if my mom was looking down from Heaven and could see how I pretty I looked.

I remember Miss Catherine Dowd, once my teacher, coming to the house with a box that contained a black dress for my sister Mary, and Mrs. Harris bought Millie a beautiful blue dress. The boys had their suits, ties, shirts, and shoes for special occasions. Yes, this was a special occasion.

When it was time for the casket to be closed, friends got up to say good-bye, and then the family members followed. With broken hearts, her children said good-bye. There were three floral pieces in the room. One floral piece was exceptionally beautiful. It was made up of red and white roses, with beautiful greens worked in around the roses and a gold ribbon that read "Love From Your Children."

We never found out who sent it. It sure was very kind of that person. We couldn't afford to buy any flowers. The casket was then placed in the hearse with the three floral pieces laid on top of it. The hearse left the farmhouse and traveled down Western Avenue and then took King Street to 9W and our beautiful St. Mary's Church.

Father Hanley walked down the church aisle to meet the casket and then gave a beautiful eulogy. He emphasized the great sacrifice that my mom had made to keep the family together. He mentioned how my brother Tony worked so hard and how later John helped with my mom and the younger siblings. The hearse left St. Mary's with a three-car procession. It seemed like a long journey as I sat in Mr. Festa's car.

As we went through town, many people stopped as we passed. I imagined that they were thinking of my mother's tragic life and how she was too young to pass on. As we headed to St. Mary's Cemetery, I got very emotional. I just couldn't handle the fact that my mom was gone.

My mother was buried with my dad in a single grave. It was a simple grave, with just brown earth and small stones covering it. The grave needed to be worked on. It had to be graded and have top soil and grass seed worked in. They were buried on the left side of the cemetery, and it seemed that they were all alone. The appearance of the grave bothered me. I didn't know when the work needed to make the grave look beautiful would take place or when we would be able to purchase a headstone. After a month passed, my brothers and their friend who had a small pickup truck loaded a bag of top soil and the tools they needed and went to work on the gravesite. Within two weeks we could see some green starting to sprout through the brown dirt. The headstone had to wait. There was just no money available for us to buy one.

After the funeral we returned home. I was overcome with sadness. The apartment was cold and empty. I had a terrible pain in my heart. How could I live without my mom's protection from Phillip?

I knew at that time that my Heavenly Mother would now also have to become my earthly mother. The thought of living without my mom was very difficult. It was not only me who felt this way but the rest of the children as well. This was especially true for Margaret and Joey, as they were the youngest. They couldn't understand why their mom was not here anymore. Phillip tried to give them more attention. Margaret, who was now five, and Joey, who was three, would cry themselves to sleep. These were very hard days to endure as children. The main person in our lives, whom we loved so much, was gone forever.

I remember I could not go into the bedroom where my mom had been laid out. The furniture was put back into the room now. But all I could picture was the casket with her frail body in it. I remember her hands the most. They were so thin and were folded together with her white rosary beads wrapped around them. The contrast of the white rosary against her blue dress was very soft. It reminded me of a pale blue sky with a touch of a thin white cloud running through it.

This was not the only room that I could not look into without feeling that wave of sadness come over me. The kitchen was the one room where she could always be found. I would picture her preparing dinner, doing laundry, or ironing our clothes. She had heated the iron on the stove until Tony and John had surprised her with an electric iron the year before her death. They were always so kind and helpful to her. They knew how sick she was and how she was forced to tolerate an abusive husband in Phillip.

At the age of eight my mom's death took a toll on me. I was unable to eat or sleep. I was just consumed with the anguish of not having her as a part of my life anymore. My teacher noticed that there was a big change in me and that I seemed very distant. She discussed this with the school nurse, Miss Stroman, who suggested that I be evaluated by a doctor. My sister Mary took me to Dr. Harris on Western Avenue. His office was located across the street from Joey's market.

Dr. Harris examined me and concluded that I was severely underweight and had anemia. He felt these conditions were results of my state of depression over the loss of my mother. I was given a tonic and other medications to help me relax and be able to sleep at night. My brother John once again took over the role of caretaker and would sometimes make me an eggnog with Ovaltine like he had once made for my mother. He was a very compassionate brother. I had to take two weeks off from school so I could rest and try to get my strength back. I was slowly improving.

Father Hanley heard about my condition and made a special trip one day to pay me a visit. He drove down to my house and spoke to me about my mom and her tragic death. He told me that my mom was now happy in Heaven because she was with the Lord, Our Blessed Mother, the Angels, and my dad. He convinced me that she was at peace. He told me that she would be praying for me and my brothers and sisters. Before he left, he gave me a special blessing. That visit was so important to me because I realized that what he had said was true. From that day on, whenever I got that sad feeling about my mom, I would think of what Father Hanley had said to me that day. God bless Father Hanley. As I think of him today, I remember him giving my mom money to buy my sister Mary a pair of glasses. I can still picture him trimming the hedges around the rectory and recall how he used to deliver long homilies. Yes, he was compassionate and caring when it came to his parishioners.

THE IMPORTANCE OF FAMILY

The situation at home was getting very troublesome. Tony and Phillip were arguing more frequently. They could not agree on paying the bills and other matters. Phillip worked at the stone crusher plant, and my brother Tony was still with DallVechia's Trucking. My brother John was still working full-time as a barber for Mr. Anthony at the shop on 9W. My brother Carmen would find small jobs to do after school.

My sister Mary did the cooking, cleaning, and laundry with help from me and Millie. Caring for Margaret and Joey, who were the youngest, also took quite a bit of our time. They were very good children.

It was now September, and my mom had been gone for two-and-a-half months. Phillip approached my sister Mary, who was now sixteen, and told her that he felt the two of them should get married. My sister was horrified. Just the thought was sickening to her. She ran immediately downstairs to my aunt Jennie and told her what Phillip had said. My aunt, who was a very tall and heavyset woman, immediately confronted him about the incident. She told him that he should be ashamed of himself for wanting to marry his sixteen-year-old stepdaughter. My aunt towered over Phillip, who was of small stature. He denied that this proposal had ever taken place and said that Mary must have had a dream. Aunt Jennie and Uncle Pete discussed the matter and decided that from then on, Mary would sleep in their apartment. They felt she would be safer at night because they would be able to watch over her.

The following day, my aunt told Phillip about their decision to have Mary sleep in their apartment at night. She would share a room with my aunt's daughters, Josephine and Annie. It would be tight until Aunt Jennie could get an additional twin bed to fit in the room, but my sister Mary was relieved that my aunt was willing to take her in. Millie and I did miss Mary at night, but we knew that her situation in our apartment had now become very uncomfortable. From that day on, the arguments between Tony and Philip and between Aunt Jennie and Philip escalated. Mary spent quite a bit of time at our aunt's home, even when she wasn't sleeping. When Phillip was at work, she helped us prepare dinner and then left to go back to my aunt's before Phillip returned. She was very uncomfortable in his presence.

Mealtime in our home had become so unpleasant. We would sit down with knots in our stomachs, not knowing when Phillip was going to explode in one of his angry tirades. One evening he came home from work really angry just as it was time to serve dinner. He greeted only Margaret and Joey with a hug. We all sat at the table except for Tony, who was still working, and of course Mary, who had already left for my aunt's apartment. We ate in silence, which was how he demanded our dinners be held. Then we ran out of bread. Italian stew requires plenty of bread to soak up the delicious flavored juice in the dish. Phillip stood up screaming and ordered Carmen to go to Fred Fowler's store to get a loaf of Italian bread. He banged his fist on the table and demanded that everyone stop eating until Carmen returned home with the bread.

Carmen ran all the way to store and back in seven minutes for fear that he was in for a beating. What a terrible night!

After a very tiresome day Millie and I climbed into bed. Sometime during the night or very early morning, Millie heard my mother's voice calling her name—"Carmela, Carmela," which is the proper name for Millie in Italian. The voice made Millie open her eyes, and there was Phillip standing over our bed. When he realized that Millie was awake, he rushed out of our room and back into his own. Millie immediately woke me up to tell me what had happened. We were so scared that we lay awake until morning. As soon as we heard Phillip leave for work, we ran to Aunt Jennie to tell her what had happened during the night.

My aunt again confronted Phillip about what had happened. He said that there was no truth to the story. My aunt knew that Millie and I were too frightened to sleep in that room. My brother Tony gave his approval for us to move our bed into the larger bedroom in my aunt's apartment. When Phillip learned about us moving out, he was furious.

It was very crowded in our new room, but we did not care because we had peace of mind.

My three brothers and Margaret and Joey remained in the apartment. It got very complicated as we sisters took care of our three brothers and of course Joey and Margaret. We still did the cleaning and cooking. Phillip was becoming more agitated as the days went on.

One day when he came home from work, he announced that he was moving out and taking Margaret and Joey with him. Mr. Festa had an empty apartment on Western Avenue. It was one in a row of four, which were referred to as the "flats."

We now all lived as a family with Aunt Jennie and Uncle Peter and our cousins. The apartment where my family had lived was now just used for bedrooms. We all ate our meals together. Our home held a total of fourteen children. The Carofano family included Peter and Jennie and their children Jennie, Katie, Rosie, Josephine, Rocky, Charles, Annie, and Antoinette; the Pascale part of the family included Tony, Mary, John, Carmen, Millie, and me, Anne. Dinners had to be prepared for sixteen people, which was not easy to do.

The atmosphere in the farmhouse was so much better after Phillip moved out, though we missed Margaret and Joey. My uncle and aunt showed us a lot of love. All of us children got along pretty well for the most part. I remember one incident when my sister Millie and cousin

Rocky were arguing over a baseball game. My sister Millie is a bona fide Yankees fan. The New York Yankees are her team. Cousin Rocky was criticizing Joe DiMaggio for a bad play that he had made, and Millie got real hot. Rocky also got hot and threw a fork at her, which stuck in her arm. She still has the scar.

My brother Tony, who was now eighteen years old, was in charge of the discipline for the children. This made things easier for my aunt and uncle. We girls argued over whose turn it was to wash the dishes, make the beds, help with the laundry, hang the clothes on the line, or wash the floor.

My cousin Jennie, who was the oldest of my aunt's children, worked in a coat factory along with Katie, who was the second-oldest. There was a big difference between Jennie and Katie. Jennie was very quiet and helped her mom a lot with the chores. Katie, on the other hand, was more active. She liked to socialize more and listen to the radio, especially to the popular songs, and dance. Katie never sat at the table for dinner. She was always on a diet even though she was tiny. She lived on green salad, rye crisps, black coffee, and vegetables. She never ate bread or sweets. She would always sneak a cigarette when my aunt wasn't around. My aunt didn't allow smoking. Rosie, the third daughter, had a completely different personality. She was an animal lover. She would milk the cow and feed the horse and chickens. Our dog, Prince, would always follow Rosie around. He definitely favored her.

Our new living quarters with my aunt and uncle included two large rooms on the first floor of the farmhouse. One was the kitchen, and the other was a dining area. The kitchen had a big black coal stove, a sink, a washing machine, and a small table to prepare the food for our dinner. The dining area had a very long narrow table with narrow chairs in to order fit everyone at dinnertime. The walls were painted a soft blue. There were no pictures on the wall except for the one of the Last Supper. When I ate my dinner, I felt like I was sitting at the Lord's Table, as it was large and colorful. There were two windows in this room with shades. The floor was grayish linoleum, and there was a small kerosene stove to use for heat when it was exceptionally cold.

Our dishes and silverware were all mismatched, with different weights and patterns. They were stored in a small built-in closet with glass doors. If you walked from the kitchen into the dining room, you would see a small radio in the corner. It was usually turned on, and we were able to listen to music or the news from all parts of the world. The room was crowded when everyone was seated at the dining room table. There was always some discussion going on about school or sports, and at times it would get very noisy when everyone tried to talk at the same time. Mealtimes were quite different from when we had lived with Phillip, when we hadn't been allowed to speak at the dinner table. It was enjoyable to be surrounded by family and to feel loved again. But I felt sad about and missed my brother Joey and sister Margaret. I wondered if they were eating well and what they were doing. It was their father's idea to move them away to the Festas' apartment.

After living in the Festas' apartment for a couple of weeks with the two children, Phillip decided that he was going to send Margaret and Joey to an orphanage. Margaret went on October 15, 1934, to St. Cabrini's, and Joey went to a foster home in Saugerties, New York, to live with the Malone family. I remember that day because it was the day that I made my confirmation.

How could one ever forget the scene from that day? A small pickup truck from social services picked up five-year-old Margaret and three-year-old Joey to take them to their new homes at their own father's request. Joey was sitting on a strange woman's lap, hysterically crying. Margaret was seated between the woman and the male driver and looked devastated and confused. I didn't know if or when I would ever see them again.

CELEBRATING CHRISTMAS

It was the beginning of December, and we were starting to feel the Christmas spirit around Marlboro. This was always a special time of year. For me it was a bittersweet time this year because it would be the first Christmas without my mom. I kept remembering this one special day before Christmas when my mom was singing Italian Christmas songs as she mixed the dough for her special Christmas cookies. The bright sun was reflecting off the clear icicles that hung from the edge of the roof, and there was snow on the ground. It was such a joyful scene. I knew I would never experience those special moments with her again. I knew I would never have those Christmas routines with my mom ever again.

For years I wondered why Santa Claus never brought me anything that I asked for. Whenever we returned to school after Christmas vacation, my classmates would tell me what Santa brought to them. I always thought that it was because I lived off Western Avenue and down a dirt road; I thought Santa didn't know where my house was. At our Christmas party in school, we would exchange names. My teacher, Miss Bewick, took the name that I picked that year, Gerard Purdy, and bought him a gift from me.

There was always a visit to the firehouse to see Santa and to get a box of Christmas hard candy that they handed out to the children from town. Father Hanley always gave a party at St. Mary's Hall too. Members of the Catholic Daughters would help prepare the goodies and serve the children. Father Hanley would ask all the children to form a circle. He would then throw coins in the air, and we would all scramble around trying to catch them. He enjoyed this as much as we did.

Another activity that my sisters, my cousins, and I enjoyed doing before Christmas was seeing the holiday decorations around town. We would walk through the neighborhood as soon as it got dark outside. Mrs. Brown, our neighbor, whose house was on Western Avenue and faced our house, always had colored lights on her shrubs and on the beautiful blue spruce tree in the center of her lawn. Many of the homes had beautiful wreaths on their doors, and a beautiful warm glow shone through their windows. Some of the homes had fireplaces with children's stockings hanging. In one of the homes there was one large stocking hanging from the mantle, and you could see the name David knitted on it in large letters. Once when we passed, we saw an older woman sitting in a rocking chair next to the fireplace, knitting what appeared to be a wool hat. I imagined it must have been David's grandmother. I thought how lucky David was to have not only a mother but also a grandmother to love and look after him.

After we were done with our tour, we would return home, make hot chocolate, and listen to the record player that one of the neighbors had handed down to us. It was rather old, but we enjoyed the Christmas carols even though the record skipped over some of the words. Our favorites were "Silent Night," "O Come, All Ye Faithful," and "Jingle Bells."

My aunt and uncle were not able to afford a Christmas gift for each of us. But they took a small brown paper bag and put some hard candy, gum, and a small sweet tangerine inside for each of us. We were satisfied with these treats, and not one of us complained. It was so wonderful just to have these two people in our lives who made us feel loved. Most of all, we felt a sense of family since my aunt was my mom's sister; it was like we still had a connection to her.

We would attend Christmas day mass at eight o'clock in the morning, and we had to fast for an hour before so that we could receive the body of Christ (communion) at mass. Father Hanley would usually have a long homily. Benediction was given at the end of every mass.

We were always anxious for mass to end so we could hurry home and enjoy the delicious pastries waiting for us, which we always had as a special treat on Christmas morning. Mr. Joe Falco, who was a dear friend of my aunt and uncle, would come in on Christmas Eve with a large white bakery box, with two layers of delicious pastries inside. I can still picture them arranged on my aunt's clear glass platter in the middle of our long dining room table. Mr. Falco would also bring a delicious traditional Italian cake large enough for the whole family. It was served after dinner and was very rich, so a small piece was sufficient.

Our Christmas dinner usually consisted of lasagna, meatballs, and sausage. We would also have baked chicken and a hearty salad mixed with my aunt's favorite dressing. She made her own vinegar, which had a very distinct taste and was so good on the salad. Our dessert was the Christmas cake, homemade cookies from Mrs. Festa, and a beautiful fruit basket sent by the Joe DallVechia family.

Christmas Eve was all Italian. The main course consisted of all types of fish. The fish was prepared in many different ways and included shrimp and plain fish fillet. Small black eels were bought and kept in a wooden tub full of water. For the next two weeks, we would feed them bread every day. The eels grew over this time and then were ready to be eaten as part of the Christmas Eve feast. My aunt would take a large butcher knife and, one by one, chop the eels in pieces. The pieces of eel would wiggle and jump around the counter. They would then be dipped in flour, to which salt, pepper, and garlic had been added. My aunt would have a large black frying pan full of olive oil already heating on the stove, ready for her to add the eels. When they were done frying, they were a toasty brown color, and the outer layer was crispy. The fish itself was moist and flavorful. It was served with an olive oil, garlic, and black pepper sauce poured over a large bowl of linguine.

This is the way we usually celebrated the Lord's birthday—with delicious pastries for breakfast and a traditional Italian dinner followed by a fantastic dessert. However, this is not how we celebrated our Christmas in December of 1934.

THE SECOND TRAGEDY

It was December 20, 1934. My aunt had gone to visit Mrs. Festa to see her newborn son Patrick. She had left the house around 6:30 p.m. and walked up the driveway and across the bridge to Western Avenue. My brother Tony was working that night, and Carmen was out visiting a friend. My uncle had promised that he would bring in the Christmas tree and that all of us children could help with the decorations. We were all very excited. We had a large windowsill on the long side of the room, and the tree was going to be placed there. It was the perfect spot because the tree would be raised from the floor, and you would see it as soon as you stepped into the room. This spot had been used for many years. My uncle came in from the cellar with a large brown box that was covered in a layer of dust. We all stood around as he opened the box and pulled out a cord that he always used to tack to the bottom of the tree in the center of the wooden post of the window. His son Rocky would tack the tree, and my uncle made sure it was centered and firm on the rusty old stand. It was then time to put the beautiful decorated balls on the tree. My uncle handed each of us one to place where we wanted. There was only one set of twenty-four lights to be used on the tree. My uncle arranged the lights so they were all on the front of the tree; this way we would be able to enjoy them. The back of the tree had no lights, but it didn't make any difference because our house was far enough from the main street that the tree couldn't be seen from Western Avenue. We begged our uncle to please keep the lights lit, as they gave the room such a beautiful glow. It was really starting to feel like Christmas now. We noticed that the garland was missing. So my uncle checked the bottom of the old dusty brown box and came up with a small string of garland and covered a few of the branches in the front of the tree. The tree was completed and looked beautiful. It was a beautiful evening too, and the ground was covered with snow from the day before, which made everything so light.

My uncle, who was a very jolly and kind person, decided that he would have an amateur hour to entertain us children. This was a fun activity for us, and we looked forward to enjoying time with my uncle. We were starting to take our places at the long dining room table when we heard our dog, Prince, start to bark. My sister Mary went into the kitchen to unlock the door. She was expecting her friend John Monahan to come for a visit that evening and thought he must have decided to visit earlier than planned. He was a local man, and they were quite friendly at that time. But when she opened the door to greet her friend John, to her surprise she was greeted with a shotgun aimed at her head instead. She screamed, and my uncle got up and hurried toward the door to see what was going on. There stood Phillip with the shotgun in his hands. When Phillip saw my uncle approaching, he moved his aim toward him. Mary ran outside into the cold dark night shaking with fear. Phillip then aimed the gun at my uncle's forehead, and a shot rang out. My uncle had raised his arm to shield his forehead just in time, and the blast hit him in the upper part of his arm. Flesh and blood immediately splattered into the air. Philip ran outside after my sister Mary. Another shot rang out, but he missed her as she turned the corner to run around the other side of the house. He then left the property and headed north in the direction of Mr. Young's property, which is where the middle school is now located.

Meanwhile, bedlam had broken out inside the house. We were all screaming and terrified because we had heard the other shot fired outside and didn't yet know Mary's fate. We feared for her life. We didn't know that she had hidden in a thicket of bushes. She later came out but was in a very bad state of shock. Having a gun aimed at her really took a toll. My uncle was in a bad state too. Part of his arm had been blown off, and he knew that he had to get himself up to Dr. Harris's office up on Western Avenue. He grabbed a towel off the counter that we used to dry the dishes and held it over his arm. He told us that we were all to go with him because he didn't know if Phillip might return to the house. We followed my uncle down the drive and over the bridge to Western Avenue. The crisp white snow, which moments before had been part of joyous Christmas spirit, was now stained red with a trail from my uncle's bleeding wound. As I walked behind my uncle, I noticed that the front of my dress was wet. I then realized that my wrist and part of my hand had been hit with pellets when Phillip shot my uncle.

My brother John had run ahead to the office to inform Dr. Harris that Uncle Pete had been shot and was on his way. The office was located in Dr. Harris's home, and John had banged on the front door until Dr. Harris came down to see what the commotion was about. When we arrived at the office, the door was open, and we entered the waiting room. My uncle went in first, leaving a trail of blood, and I followed behind him. I remember my uncle saying in Italian, "That traitor came into my house and did this." Immediately Dr. Harris tied his arm with a rubber tube and told us that he was going to drive my uncle to St. Luke's Hospital in Newburgh. He instructed his wife, who was a nurse, to attend to my hand. He would check on me when he returned from the hospital.

While the doctor was driving my uncle to the hospital, one of the neighbors notified Mrs. Festa that Pete had been shot. My aunt, who was at the Festas' house, was horrified by the news. Mr. Festa drove my aunt to the hospital so that she could be with her husband. When she walked into my uncle's room, he told her not to worry and that he was going to be all right. That was a big relief to my aunt.

When Dr. Harris returned from the hospital, he tended to my hand. It was still bleeding but not as profusely as it had been before Mrs. Harris put compresses on it. The bleeding was near the vein. Dr. Harris put ointment and a very tight bandage on it. I was then able to leave and return to the house. My brother John had waited with me, and we walked home through the darkness of night together. It was sure frightening. My aunt remained at the hospital to be at her husband's bedside. As we walked toward the farmhouse, we noticed that all the lights in the kitchen and the dining room were off. It was in one of the back bedrooms that we found everyone huddled together with the light of just one small lamp. They were hiding in fear that Phillip might come back.

The Kingston State Troopers had been notified about the shooting by the head doctor at St. Luke's. The law required that any kind of gun injury be reported to the authorities. Since the shooting had taken place in Ulster County, the Kingston State Troopers were called in. We were informed that Sergeants Lockhart and Baker were on the case, so we were somewhat relieved. We stayed in the bedroom until 2:00 a.m., when we received the news that Phillip had been caught near St. Mary's Cemetery. We were so relieved by his capture. The troopers came to our house after Phillip had been placed in the courthouse on King Street in Marlboro. They told us that he was captured while sitting alongside Mr. Frank Felicello on his horse and wagon. When the troopers surrounded him, they ordered him to get out of the seat with his hands up. He didn't have much chance to do anything because the troopers had their guns aimed at him. The first question he asked the troopers was, "Did he die?" He was referring to my uncle Pete.

Mr. Felicello had been at home when Phillip entered his house on the back roads of Marlboro and ordered him to take him to the train station or he would shoot him. The shooting had taken place around 7:00 p.m., and he was captured by the troopers at 2:00 a.m.

The following day, Phillip was taken to the Kingston jail from the courthouse on King Street in Marlboro. It was a very brisk morning. We stood with a small crowd that had gathered outside the courthouse to get a glimpse of him as he was put into the troopers' car. Troopers Lockhart and Baker parked their shiny black car in front of the wooden courthouse and stood erect as they exited their car. Their wide-brimmed trooper's hats didn't budge as they made their entrance to the building. The crowd of people waited anxiously to see the reaction on Phillip's face. This was a major event in this small farming community. Marlboro was a very quiet and friendly town. When he exited the courthouse, he was flanked by the two state troopers, and his face showed no sign of remorse.

Our neighbor Rose Affuso had told me to show Phillip my bandaged hand to let him know that I had been injured, but I refused to. He really didn't know that I had been injured, as my injury had been caused by a pellet that was part of the spray of gunfire intended for my uncle.

We all felt confident that my uncle was going to pull through, but Phillip had made sure that whoever was shot would not live. He had added pieces of metal and glass and other ingredients to the bullet powder. These foreign particles would cause a very powerful infection in a human's body. His plan worked—some of the pellets lodged in my uncle's lungs and caused an infection that quickly spread through his body. The hospital was unable to treat the infection because there was no penicillin available in 1934.

When the troopers searched Phillip's apartment, they noticed that the floorboards in his sitting room had been disturbed. When they investigated, they found that he had stored seventy-one sticks of dynamite under the floorboards. We never found out what he had intended to use the dynamite for. Since he worked at the stone crusher, it was easy to get his hands on them. In the apartment where he lived there were five adjoining apartments. They were home to families with many children. The large Festa house included four families and was right next door to where the dynamite was concealed. On the other side of the five-room apartment building was a building that held the first and second grades of the Marlboro School District.

What did he have in mind? A week after the shooting took place, Mr. Young, who owned the apple orchard where the middle school now exists, discovered three loaded guns, ammunition, and a professional razor. This was the direction Phillip had run after the shooting. After much investigating, Philip admitted that he owned the guns, ammunition, and razor. He had dropped them, as it was too much of a burden to carry them while he was fleeing.

THE AFTERMATH

My uncle passed away at 4:55 p.m. on December 21, twenty-two hours and five minutes after he was shot. He was forty-eight years old and left behind his wife and eight children and six nieces and nephews. It was a tragic day for Marlboro as the news spread of his death. He was such a well-liked man.

My aunt was put under the doctor's care. She had expected her husband to pull through even though part of his arm had been blown off at close range.

What was Phillip's motive for the shooting? Was it payback time because my sister Mary wouldn't marry him? Is that why he aimed the gun at her? Was my uncle shot because he'd kept his promise to my mom as she lay dying to take care of her children? My uncle passed away six months after my mom. We all now had to face the fact that my uncle was gone. We all had to band together and give my aunt all the support she needed.

On the evening of my uncle's death, we worked together to take down the Christmas tree that he so joyfully had set up on the windowsill just twenty-four hours earlier. My uncle had been standing only about three feet from the Christmas tree when he was shot, and we were not able to save any of the beautiful balls that we had hung on the tree. The branches and balls were splattered with my uncle's blood, and pieces of flesh from his partly blown-off arm hung from the branches. The decorations were put back into the old dusty brown box and removed from the room to be discarded. There were pellet holes in the ceiling of the room. They were eventually painted over, but the holes still remained for as long as I can remember. The following morning, my aunt and uncle's bedroom was cleaned out in order to place the casket there for the viewing.

Mr. Tuthill came to pick up his suit, shirt, tie, and shoes. He told my aunt that he would have to stuff my uncle's sleeve where the part of his arm was missing. I remember that at the viewing there were dark gloves on both my uncle's hands too.

The viewing hours spanned two days. It seemed like the whole town shuffled through the room to pay their respects, and he received many floral pieces. His relatives who lived in New Jersey all attended, and friends from Poughkeepsie whom he first met when he came from Italy visited too. The local businesses also contributed money for the funeral, including Fred Fowler, Jim's Meat Market, Barkley Drug Store, Fromels's ice cream parlor, and Mondello's Restaurant. Although my uncle was not a fireman, the firemen showed up as a unit and paid their respects. One floral piece remains in my mind as if I saw it yesterday. It was placed on the right side of the casket. It was circular with beautiful red and white roses and greens arranged in between. In the center was a small clock, and the hands were set to 4:55, his time of death. This floral piece was given by the Italian American club of which he was a member. My uncle had one of the largest, greatest funerals in town.

On the day of the funeral, the Italian American club members along with their marching band walked from my uncle's home to Western Avenue to King Street and onto 9W to St. Mary's Church. The officers of the club led the cortege with the American flag and the Italian-American flag.

My aunt followed in Joe DallVechia's black car with her three daughters, Jennie, Rosie, and Katie. Joe had graciously volunteered to drive them.

The Italian American club members lined up on each side of the steps leading into the church. Members of the club carried the casket, with my aunt and her daughters following behind. The organist played "Ave Maria," and my aunt, overcome by grief, had to be revived. Father

Hanley gave a beautiful eulogy. He mentioned how my uncle had kept his promise at his sister-in-law's bedside as she was dying and had taken care of her children. He was a very hardworking man who labored at the stone crusher and on the weekends on the farm with his two sons. After the funeral mass the Italian American club took their places in the procession. As they drove through the village, many people stopped to nod their heads out of respect for the family. It was a very sad scene. The hearse continued to St. Mary's Cemetery. The graves were all decorated for Christmas; it was Christmas Eve.

We returned home from the cemetery to our sad and lonely house. My aunt had to be helped out of the car. We sat her down once we got into the house. Dr. Harris had prescribed some medication for her. Her daughter Jennie gave her a glass of water with two pink pills that seemed to relax her.

While we were at the funeral mass and cemetery, the kitchen table had been stacked full of food. There was a large roasted turkey, a large ham, potatoes, vegetables, and in a covered gravy bowl, delicious gravy for the turkey. Pies and a large fruit basket were in the center. The food had all been donated by the local businesses. The DallVechias had sent the fruit basket, and Mrs. Festa had prepared her famous assorted cookies. What gracious people. They were always there when needed.

A week later my hand was not healed and was giving me a lot of trouble. I was very uncomfortable in the classroom, as I was unable to write since it was my right hand that was injured. My teacher, Miss Catherine Dowd, had to give my tests and homework to me orally. She was a loving and compassionate teacher. God bless her soul!

The pain was unbearable, and large amounts of pus kept draining. Dr. Harris was very concerned. The infection was going up my arm and had reached my elbow. Dr. Harris tried different ointments and a soaking solution, but there was no improvement. His fear was that my arm would have to be amputated up to my elbow.

He called a specialist in one of the New York City hospitals who prescribed a different solution, and within a week there was so much improvement. Dr. Harris was pleased with my recovery. He told me that I was very lucky, as I had just a small amount of the tainted bullet powder that Phillip had concocted. On the other hand, my uncle had had a very large amount in his body, especially in his lungs where the pellets had sprayed.

Jennie Carofano Buccieri

THE HEARING

A COUPLE OF MONTHS LATER, a hearing was held at the Kingston Courthouse. Four of us children were called to a private hearing in front of the judge who was presiding over the case. We were escorted by two police officers into a large room, where we saw many brown leather chairs lined in rows across the room. On the right side of the courtroom stood our beautiful American flag. Sitting in front was a stenographer recording our testimony. The defense lawyers, appointed by the court, were Mr. George Rusk and his partner Mr. Conway. They were seated in the front row.

When Judge Russell walked into the room, everyone stood up, and we said the Pledge of Allegiance. As soon as that was done, Phillip was escorted into the room, flanked by two officers. He was wearing his brown suit, and he looked exhausted. He definitely was not remorseful. I had promised myself that I wouldn't look at him, but I just couldn't resist watching him as he walked across the room and took a seat next to the attorney George Rusk. I was nine years old at the time. I was the first to be called up, and I took a seat next to Judge Russell's desk. The first thing I noticed was a photo of our dining room where the shooting had taken place. It seemed confusing to me until a court officer adjusted it. The judge asked me, "Where was your uncle standing at the time he was shot?" I slowly pointed to the spot in the photo leading from the kitchen to the dining room. I was then asked, "Where was Mr. Deciano standing at the time he shot your uncle, Mr. Carofano?" He was standing at the entrance of the dining room and the kitchen, I explained. They were face to face.

Next the judge asked, "Do you know what a lie is?"

"If you lie, you're going down there," I answered quietly, pointing toward the floor, "and burn." There was a large roar of laughter in the room. Even Judge Russell broke a smile. Later Millie and Josephine testified and were also asked similar questions. The courtroom was filled to capacity. Many Marlboro residents attended, as it was a great tragedy to happen in a small friendly town. Charges of first-degree murder were brought against Phillip Deciano after a hearing before the grand jury. This charge was later withdrawn when it was determined that Phillip was criminally insane. The defense stated that he had been gassed in World War I when fighting in Italy.

He was sent to the Matteawan State Hospital in Beacon, New York, without any chance of ever being released. My aunt and other family members were very disappointed in the verdict but had to accept it.

The following spring, Mother's Day came, and I was so upset because I wanted so much to adorn my mother's grave site with flowers, but I had no money for flowers, and I did not have a vase to use either. Then a thought came into my mind. I went into the cellar to look for a pint jar that my mom had used to can tomatoes. I finally found one beneath the storing shelves. It was covered with dust, so I rushed to the sink and washed it with an old bottle brush and some dried-up soap from under the sink. It looked pretty good. I then filled it with water and set out to look for some wild flowers. I found some beautiful yellow and lavender wild spring flowers and arranged them in the tomato jar. I made sure that the flowers were positioned firmly in the jar, as there was always a wind at St. Mary's Cemetery. Mrs. Festa always went to the cemetery on Mother's Day. I had asked her the day before if I could ride with her so I could visit my mom and dad's grave. She was more than happy to take me. I placed the jar at the head of the grave and arranged some small stones around it to keep it in place.

On this visit, I felt so much better about the appearance of the grave site. The green grass was now almost covering the area, and it made such a nice contrast with the yellow and lavender flowers. I said the Our Father, Hail Mary, and Glory Be and said to my mom and dad, "I love you, and I miss you." As I walked away, I noticed that the birds were singing.

I learned in later years that Phillip lived at Matteawan for approximately thirty years before he passed away. His two children, Margaret and Joey, were not aware of their father's crime until they were older.

Margaret and Joey

Margaret spent eleven years at St. Cabrini's Orphanage until my sister Mary got her released at the age of sixteen. Mary, who was now married to Frank Falco from Long Island, had decided it was time for her to live with family. Her husband was very much in favor, and they started the proceedings to get custody of Margaret from St. Cabrini's. She would be coming into a beautiful family life and would get to meet her niece and nephews. My sister at the time had three children, Tommy, Michael, and Gracie Ann, and they were very excited about the new addition.

Mary and Frank made an appointment to discuss the procedures for Margaret to come and live with them. They left one morning very early, as the trip from their house would take at least three hours. As they drove on 9W, they saw the sign for West Park and looked for St. Cabrini's Orphanage on the right side. Minutes later they arrived at the orphanage. As they entered, they saw a beautiful statue of the Blessed Mother on the right, and to the left there was a space to park.

There stood this large red brick building. They went toward it and climbed the stairs to the entrance. On the right of the huge brown door was the doorbell. The sound of the bell could be heard all around the building. It seemed to take a long time for someone to answer the door. As they waited, Mary felt butterflies in her stomach. The door was opened by a Catholic nun who introduced herself as Sister Rose. The sister was dressed in the traditional black habit, with her black rosary beads hanging at her side and swaying as she moved.

She invited them in, and they entered a side room, where they were told to sit. They spoke about Margaret, and Sister Rose explained there were forms to be filled out when a child was removed from the orphanage. There would have to be an investigation about my sister and her husband, and then it would have to be approved by the board. The nun gave the forms to my sister, who neatly folded them and put them in her purse. Sister Rose then brought them to Margaret's classroom and had Margaret excused from the class. They went to the library where it was empty, and Margaret hugged my sister; she remembered her from previous visits.

Sister Rose asked Margaret, "How would you like to live with your sister Mary?"

Margaret's face lit up with a smile and sparkling eyes, and she responded, "I would be very happy." My sister gave Margaret a kiss and another big hug.

Margaret was a very sweet girl. She had beautiful black curly hair and brown eyes. She was dressed in a brown dress that came down below her knee, brown tied shoes, and white knee socks. Margaret then had to return to her classroom. She embraced my sister and her husband, Frank. Sister Rose explained to Mary that they would investigate her husband's salary and asked whether Margaret would complete her senior year and graduate and whether the family attended Sunday mass. Sister Rose said that Margaret would be able to leave in a week if everything was approved. All the notarized forms were completed and returned to Sister Rose.

In June 1945 Mary and Frank received a phone call reporting the board's approval. Before the trip to West Park to pick up Margaret, my sister went clothes shopping for Margaret's homecoming. She bought her a beautiful blue dress, white shoes and socks, and other necessities. Mary and Frank left Long Island with their hearts full of joy and happiness. They were very excited as they parked their car and approached the red brick building. They carried the beautiful clothes that Margaret would wear in a different atmosphere, one of family life. Her life in the orphanage had lasted from age five to sixteen. After they walked up the stairs to the huge front door, Frank hit the bell button. It sure was loud and clear, and the sound had a joyful sound to it. Yes, Margaret was leaving the orphanage and coming to her new home. Sister Rose answered the door with a beautiful bright smile and asked them to please come in. She brought them to a beautiful room where Margaret was waiting with a huge smile and open arms. She was wearing the same brown dress, tied brown shoes, and white knee socks as before.

My sister asked Sister Rose if Margaret could change into the dress and shoes she had purchased. Sister Rose said this would be fine, so Margaret went into a different room to change into her new clothes. When she came out all dressed up, she looked like a princess. The blue dress brought out her beautiful brown curly hair and her deep brown eyes. The dowdy look of her brown dress was gone, and she now had the look of a shining star. Margaret and Sister Rose said their good-byes as they walked down the hall to the front entrance. Sister Rose then walked Margaret to the car, and they hugged each other as Frank opened the back door to let Margaret in. Sister Rose, with tears in her eyes, said, "God bless you."

My sister Mary and her husband got into the car and sat in their seats for a bit before starting the car. They watched Sister Rose return to the red brick building dressed in her black habit, her black rosary around her waist again swaying as she climbed the stairs and entered through the huge brown door.

Frank started up the car and left the parking area of the orphanage, passing the beautiful statue of the Blessed Mother, and then made a left turn onto 9W.

Margaret was in a trance as they drove to Long Island and her new home. When they passed the town of Marlboro, Mary told her that this was her birthplace and that she had lived there for five years before her dad put her in St. Cabrini's.

My sister's three children were waiting to meet Margaret. They were very excited to meet the new addition to the family. As they heard the car enter their driveway, they all ran to the large picture window in the living room to see her. They watched her get out of the car, and Gracie Ann commented on how pretty Margaret was as she entered the door to the living room. Margaret seemed a bit confused by the warm greeting she got from her niece and nephews. But she finally had a happy look as they all hugged her and introduced themselves. They couldn't wait to show her her bedroom. She was so delighted at the beautiful room that she could call her own. She especially loved the printed yellow spread and the lovely curtains that matched on the two windows on each side of the room. On the walls, which were painted off-white, hung two pictures with white wooden frames and a yellow background. One showed a teenage girl with dark hair and smiling eyes, and the other was a teenage girl sitting in a chair reading a book. These pictures sure complemented the beautiful spread and curtains. On her white dresser sat a picture of Our Lady of Fatima on the left and a picture of the Sacred Hear of Jesus on the right. These pictures made her feel at home because St. Cabrini's Orphanage was Catholic, although many no-Catholic children were there.

There was one more surprise for Margaret—her clothes closet. Gracie Anne opened the closet door, and Margaret happily said, "Wow." Her dresses were all hung on beautiful satin hangers. At the floor of the closet were two pairs of shoes and a pair of white sneakers. My sister knew that Margaret would need the sneakers for gym when she went to school.

Gracie Anne then opened the drawers to the dresser. There lay folded all of Margaret's pajamas, sweaters, and undergarments. In a smaller drawer in the dresser were all her socks in assorted colors. Margaret was overwhelmed by everything.

My sister was now preparing dinner. Gracie Anne and Margaret decided to help in setting the table. My sister made an Italian dinner, of course; it was spaghetti and meatballs and a hearty salad of romaine lettuce, purple onion, tomatoes, and black olives from her garden, served with a blend of aged vinegar, olive oil, garlic powder, salt, and black pepper. Their desert was cannoli from Dino's Bakery. Margaret was somewhat hesitant about the cannoli filling, as she had never had it before, but once she tasted it, that was the end of the cannoli. Wine was served for Frank, and my sister and the children had soda and water was for my sister. Margaret got soda, as they very seldom had it at the orphanage.

Before their dinner Margaret gave a blessing: "Thank you, Lord, for my beautiful family and home." For one second, Mary was lost in deep thought at the end of the dinner table as she looked at Margaret. She remembered my mom saying to her that Margaret and Joey were the same to her as were her Pascale children.

After dinner they sat in the living room for a short time, and Margaret opened up about her life in the orphanage. She just remembered that everything had changed for her so quickly. She was no longer in her bed at the home she knew but on a small bed with many other small beds in this large room. All the children ate in this large room, and they were not able to speak to each other or make any noise during mealtime.

She then asked how many sisters and brothers she had. They told her four brothers and three sisters. "Why was I put in the orphanage?" she asked. Mary tried to explain to her as gently as she could. She told Margaret that one brother had the same last name as she did. His name was Joey, and he had been put in a foster home. Mary then told her that we all had the same mother but different fathers and that it was her father who had removed Joey and her from the rest of the family, the Pascales.

Two weeks later, Mary and Frank took Margaret to visit her brother Joey in Saugerties at the residence of Joey's foster parents. He had been with this family since he and Margaret were first taken away. Mary got the directions from my brother John.

When they arrived, they parked their car and went up to the front door. The foster mother answered the door, and Mary said that they would like to meet with Joey Deciano. The foster mother was very gracious and said that she would get him; he was playing with her sons in the back of her house in an empty lot.

Within minutes Joey came to the front of the house with the other boys. He was a complete stranger. He didn't know them or anything about us. He had gone to this foster home when he was only three years old. His foster mother explained to him that we were part of his family. He was very shy. We didn't explain to him that he and Margaret had the same last name. It was decided to leave all the explaining for a later date when he was older. He was thirteen years old at this time. More visits were needed before he was told anything of the terrible past.

Margaret later asked Mary about her (Margaret's) father. Then followed questions of why he had placed her brother in a foster home and her in an orphanage. Mary told her that he was a very sick man with a sick mind and that he was now in a hospital. She said that she would go into further detail another day.

The next day Margaret and her nieces and nephews took a walk around the neighborhood. She met some of their friends, and they were all very pleasant to her, which made her very happy. This was her first opportunity to be out and about without being confined to a building with many rules. They were very strict with the children at the orphanage.

September was just around the corner, and Mary had to enroll Margaret in school. Margaret attended the Jamaica High School, and the following year, she graduated with honors. She had a good educational foundation from the orphanage.

She next enrolled in a community college, where she took up business and marketing. After her graduation she was hired by the Green Bus Lines in the business office. She adjusted to her new life rather quickly. She was doing quite well and liked her job. After working there for a year, she met mechanic Carl Hager, who was supervisor of all the Green Line buses. They courted for a year and then married. They bought a home in Elmont, Long Island.

Shortly after her marriage to Carl, Margaret decided to visit her father. When she got to Matteawan State Hospital in Beacon, she was told that he was deceased. She seemed very disappointed, but she had never seemed interested in visiting him when she lived with my sister Mary. Margaret then asked if she could visit Phillip's grave. After much searching and investigating, they were unable to locate the grave. It was a very disappointing day for Margaret.

Margaret later learned that her father didn't have a grave. When Philip passed, a phone call had been made to the Carofano/Pascale residence about what arrangements the family wanted to make for the body. Kate Carofano answered the phone and told them, "Burn the son of a bitch!" Evidently he was cremated, and that was the end, as there were no ashes.

Margaret and Carl had four children, two boys and two girls. The two girls and one of the sons live on Long Island; the other son lives in Virginia.

My sister Margaret was a very heavy smoker. She died at the age of fifty from a massive heart attack. Her husband Carl remarried shortly after her death. He passed away in 2009.

This was the brief history of my sister Margaret, who had everything to live for but went to the Lord at the age of fifty. God bless you, Margaret, for being such a wonderful sister who endured much suffering for eleven years! You're now with your mom, who you knew for only less than five years.

My brother Joey left his foster home at the age of eighteen and joined the Navy. He remembered my brother John well as John would visit him at the foster home. So on one of his furloughs from the Navy, he stopped to visit his siblings. He initially was very shy at this meeting but then started to warm up. He wanted to know more about the family.

John explained to him that we had the same mom but a different father and tried to explain that after our mom's death, things between his father and us siblings were not working out. His father had then decided to move out. He had placed Joey in a foster home at the age of three and Margaret in an orphanage at the age of five. We told Joey that his sister Margaret had spent eleven years at St. Cabrini's Orphanage before my sister had taken her out to live with her and her family in Long Island. He was anxious to see her again after five years. Before his furlough was up, he wanted to see his father too.

There was still a week left before he had to return to the Navy. We decided first to visit his sister and spend the day. We left very early in the morning and arrived within two and a half hours. We parked the car on the road in front of Mary's house, and as we were getting out of the car, we saw Margaret standing in the doorway. She came forward and put her arms around him, and they looked at each other with a smile, but they seemed rather awkward. At the time they met, he was nineteen, and she was twenty-one. The last time they had lived together as a family, she was five and he was three. It was as though they were meeting for the first time. We all had tears in our eyes, for at last they were together. Imagine how these children suffered all those years missing their mother and siblings.

My sister Mary prepared a beautiful dinner. While the dessert was being served, I asked Joey what his years in his foster home had been like. He said that was the only life he knew. He didn't remember his life with his mom, dad, and siblings, and he had spent fifteen years with the Malone family. He didn't want to talk about his life in the foster home at that time. He wanted to know more about his mom and dad and what they were like. Mary told him about mom first. She said Mom had been very sick for a long time. After she visited many doctors and underwent surgery, her condition worsened. And she went home with the Lord. His eyes were teary, and then he asked if we had a picture of her. My sister did have one picture in her album. She took it out and handed it to him. He stared at it and kissed it. Mary said she would have a copy made for him. He thought that I resembled our mother.

Then came the delicate story of his father. He wanted to know everything in detail, including why he was in Matteawan State Hospital for the Criminally Insane. My brother John told him that Phillip had a sick mind and on December 21, 1934, he had gone to the home of his brother-in-law, Peter Carofano, and shot him. Peter died the following day. A hearing was held and Phillip was declared criminally insane. He was then sent to the Matteawan State Hospital for the Criminally Insane.

Joey became distraught upon hearing this information. He couldn't believe that his father was a murderer. He then started to open up about his life at the foster home. His life at first had been very unpleasant until he got older. The foster mother had two biological sons, and they had special privileges. He was forbidden to open the refrigerator or have snacks when her sons were granted this privilege, for example. When he got older and attended the Saugerties school system, things seemed to get better. He made friends and played sports.

When Joey no longer lived with his foster parents and was out on his own, he kept in touch with the Malone family. He never forgot his foster mother's birthday, Mother's Day, or Christmas. There were always flowers or a gift for her. He also kept in touch with her two sons. That was the only family he had known growing up. But now he had gotten to meet his real sister and half-siblings and was looking forward to meeting his real father.

Gaye Festa VanEtten, my dear friend and daughter of our neighbors, the Festas, drove Joey, who was wearing his Navy uniform, to visit Phillip. They drove down 9W to Newburgh and then took the Newburgh-Beacon ferry to Beacon. There was then a short trip to the Matteawan State Hospital. Gaye wore her black suit. Her beautiful shiny black hair was styled with bangs that reached the top of her dark eyes. Her deep red lipstick complemented this look.

They parked the car in a visitor's space and walked toward the entrance of the building. There were bars covering the windows. Two guards met them as they entered and directed them to a small room. They were asked whom they were there to visit. Joey answered, "My father, Phillip Deciano." They asked Gaye if she was related to Phillip too, and she said no, but Phillip was her neighbor for some years. She explained that she had driven Joey to visit his father because Joey didn't have a car.

After more questions were answered, two guards walked them to a visitor's room; Phillip was already seated, and when his son was brought in, he stood up and shook his hand. He seemed very confused but proud. He asked him how many years he'd been in the Navy. Joey answered, "Just one year. I joined when I was eighteen."

Phillip then looked up at Gaye and said, "You're Jimmy Festa's daughter?" He recognized her. She was only eight years old the last time he had seen her. Phillip had a good memory. After their brief visit Joey left with a sad look on his face. His mom was gone, he told Gaye, and he'd never gotten to meet her except by going to the cemetery to say a prayer. "My father is in this institution," he said. "I spent fifteen years in a foster home thinking I would be part of their family."

Joey was happy to have met his sister and his half-brothers and half-sisters. But his furlough would end in three days, and he now wanted to spend some more time with his foster family and some of his friends in Saugerties. My brother John drove him to Saugerties that day. Before they left, we hugged him, and he said, "I will stop in on my next furlough." He is just a beautiful person. As I write this part of my book, I can't help but feel the lonely part of his life when he was taken away from us. He was the baby, and we all loved him dearly.

When his time was over in the Navy, Joey made his home in Saugerties. This was the only home and family that he had known. He later married Anne Hager. She was a very sweet girl, and we were happy to have her join our family. Their family consisted of three daughters and a son. After many years they divorced. He then moved to Florida, where he met and married Margaret. She's a very religious person and takes good care of Joey.

My sisters and I are very close to Joey. My brother John remained close to him also. Joey visits his daughters, who live in Saugerties, two or three times a year. At every visit he makes sure to stop to visit my sister Millie and me. He's now seventy-five years old, and his health is failing. There's not been one birthday on which he's failed to call me or one Christmas on which he hasn't sent me a card. He always signs it, "I love you, Annie."

Barn Fire

I T WAS SPRINGTIME IN 1935, and there was plenty of work on the farm. The younger boys, Rocky and Charlie, typically worked after school for a few hours. My brother Carmen played sports, especially basketball, and he helped work on the farm on weekends.

I remember Marlboro playing our rivals, Highland. To us it was like the New York Yankees playing the Boston Red Sox. My brother was considered a hero at one particular game. He scored a basket in the last seven seconds of the game, and Marlboro beat Highland by two points that night and won the championship.

I remember the players picking my brother up and the fans cheering for a good, full minute. The bleachers were being stomped so hard that the sound carried out through the gym, and our school band played the alma mater. My brother was a junior at the time and planned to remain in school and graduate, which he did.

Cousins Rocky and Charlie decided to quit school to help their mom, my aunt Jennie, on the farm. After my uncle's death, my aunt worked very hard on the farm with the help of a farmhand. Her health was starting to fail; she required more rest.

At this time, my brother Tony was still working for DallVechia trucking. My brother John was a full-time barber, and cousin Josephine worked in a coat factory. Millie, Annie, and I were still in school. That year I remember my aunt was so upset because it was a very bad season for the farm, as there was an extreme lack of rain. This was the first season since my uncle passed that she didn't have the interest money to pay Mr. Charles Brown the $120 she owed twice a year on her mortgage. "Mr. Charlie," as my aunt called him, always liked the payments on time. Rather than approach Mr. Brown and ask him if the mortgage payment could wait until strawberry season, she borrowed the money from Mr. Festa. That upcoming season was a good one. There was an abundance of strawberries to be picked. The first profit was paid to Mr. Festa in the amount of $120.

There was a lot of stress on my aunt associated with the outgoing bills and having to depend on the crops to bring a good income. Property taxes, fuel costs, medical expenses, the cost of materials for the farm such as spray for the fruit trees, and other household expenses were overwhelming her. She was unable to work on the farm anymore, and the income brought in by Tony, John, and cousin Josephine was not enough to cover the expenses.

We finally had a high school graduate, and that was my sister Millie at age sixteen-and-a-half. After the graduation ceremony, the receiving line was set up in the cafeteria. All the tables and chairs were removed, and there was ample room for the graduates. Most of the girls had bouquets of flowers waiting for them, sent in by their families. Millie knew that there would be no flowers waiting for her, and she felt down about it. She was so surprised when a beautiful basket of flowers was presented to her from Mr. and Mrs. Joe DallVechia. That meant so much to her. She also received monetary gifts from her elementary teachers, Miss Dowd and Miss Bewick.

One beautiful June evening, while Millie was attending the junior prom, my cousins Josephine, Anne, and Charlie and I were on the porch, and we invited Dominic, the farmhand, to join us. Dominic started to tell us of his childhood and how he had become a loner after his girlfriend left him after all the wedding plans were made. He then left teary-eyed and very sad. As he walked back to the barn, he lit a cigarette. We could see the light of his cigarette as he entered the barn. His mattress was on the upper floor, so he had to pass the horse and a pile of hay before going up the stairs. He always carried a flashlight to guide him in the dark barn. We had just stepped back inside the house when we heard the fire sirens. We all went outside and saw flames coming out of the barn. We realized that Dominic must have thrown his cigarette butt on the ground, thinking it was completely out. When the firemen arrived, we told them that there was a man and a horse in the barn. They dowsed the barn, but it was too late. The horse was dead. On the top floor they found Dominic's body next to a window.

It was completely charred. After the investigation it was concluded that the fire had started where the pile of hay was stored.

We were all very saddened by this tragedy. The barn was then rebuilt. This was another expense to be added to my aunt's mortgage.

Another Life Changing Decision

Since there was no money for college, my sister Millie got a job in a Newburgh coat factory. I remember her buying me my first Easter suit. Millie also contributed toward the household expenses. We all felt very bad for my aunt, given this heavy burden she had to carry.

One day one of our cousins, Rose Cioffi from Connecticut, came to visit. She didn't make this trip too often. She was fifty years old and very stern-looking. This was just a friendly visit, but she was upset by how my aunt looked. She felt my aunt needed more help with the farm. Out of the clear blue sky, Rose mentioned she knew a widower from her town. My aunt felt very uncomfortable with the conversation but was courteous enough to hear Rose out. After much persuasion she agreed to meet him.

My cousin returned with the widower, Louis Buccieri, on the following Sunday. We children were all excited. We waited patiently on the concrete porch in front of the farmhouse. It was 11:30 a.m. when we saw a gray Ford making a left turn onto our drive from Western Avenue. It traveled down the hill and over the bridge and pulled to a stop in front of the house.

Louis got out of the car and came around the opposite side to open the passenger door to let cousin Rose out. Rose introduced Louis to my aunt Jennie. It was a beautiful Sunday morning, and Louis had come dressed in his best clothes. He was wearing a pair of well-pressed gray pants, a white shirt with an open collar, and white shoes. With his attire, he seemed out of place on the farm. My aunt, who was a gracious and humble person, was wearing a fine blue print dress, and her salt-and-pepper hair was pulled back into a bun. She welcomed him with a smile on her blushed face. She asked him in for coffee, and we all followed. Tony was not present because he was working; of the boys in the family, only my cousins Rocky and Charlie were there. Louis also had a teenage son named Anthony who had remained at home with his sister, Theresa. The following weekend, Louis brought his son with him. He wanted him to get acquainted with "the boys." All of these boys seemed to enjoy each other's company. After a six-month courtship, my aunt Jennie and Louis got married. My aunt was no longer Jennie Carofano but Jennie Buccieri.

Things went very smoothly at first. Mortgage payments, taxes, and expenses were taken care of. School was about to open for the fall, and Louis was going to drive us to Newburgh to get our school clothes. My sister Millie, my cousins, and I got into the backseat of the gray Ford. My aunt sat in the front with her pocketbook and a small black purse that contained the money she had put aside for our clothes. This money was usually saved at the end of the summer when all the fruit was picked and sold. Thank God it had been a fruitful season. It was much better than last year when my aunt had been left in debt.

We were all packed in the back like sardines, but we didn't mind because we were very excited that we were going to get new clothes. As we drove down 9W to Newburgh, Aunt Jennie and Uncle Louis were discussing their financial matters. They were speaking in Italian, but I could understand what they were saying. They were talking about how they had enough money to pay the interest on the mortgage, land and school taxes, insurance, and other yearly expenses.

They were done with their conversation as we entered Water Street in Newburgh where all the department stores were. Both Schoonmaker's and Penney's were here. Schoonmaker's was the more expensive of the two stores. Uncle Louis tried to get a parking place near Penney's so my aunt wouldn't have to walk too far, as she was having trouble with her legs. Her elastic stockings helped the pain somewhat, but she had to sit often to take the pressure off of her legs. Uncle Louis parked the car, and we all jumped out.

When we entered the store, we immediately started looking through the racks for our size dresses. We were allowed three dresses each. My aunt sat in a chair near the fitting room. It didn't take us too long to pick out what we liked, as they had just gotten a new shipment. There was one problem: Millie and I picked out the same dress. One of us had to give the dress up. My aunt said that since Millie was older, I would have to pick a different one. Going through the racks again, I picked out a beautiful green dress with small white flowers that I liked better. We girls now were all done picking out our dresses. We then went to the sweater, shoes, socks, and underwear departments. When we were done shopping, we carried our items to the counter and register. It took twelve minutes to calculate the total. When my aunt was told the total of the bill, she graciously took her little black purse out of her pocketbook and counted out the money. The money was rolled in twenties, tens, and fives. She was very careful as she handed the amount to the cashier.

It was quite tiresome doing all that shopping. But since my aunt had sat while we were picking out our clothes, her legs were not bothering her. Our clothes filled the trunk of the car. It was past noontime, and we were all hungry. I asked my aunt if we could go to Texas Wieners on Broadway for a hot dog with their delicious sauce. To my surprise, Uncle Louis said it would be okay.

The soda bottles at Texas Wieners were sixteen ounces, and I asked the waitress for some paper cups so we could share. She then brought three bottles of Coke with six paper cups, which were followed by six delicious hot dogs, with the sauce dripping over the side of the bun. We couldn't wait to devour them. After we all finished, Uncle Louis left a medium tip.

As we were walking out, I met Gaye Festa with her mom and dad. Gaye also was clothes shopping, but she didn't shop at any department store. The Hilda Shop was a very expensive store that sold designer clothes, and Gaye always had the best of everything. My aunt and Nettie Festa greeted each other on our way out to the car. We all got settled in the backseat again, and we were very talkative on the way home about our new clothes and what we were going to wear on the first day of school.

As soon as we reached the farmhouse, we all got out and waited for Uncle Louis to open the trunk of the car. The first thing he did was help my aunt out of the car and into the comfortable club chair in the house, after which he put a stool at the end of the chair so she could rest her legs. He then came out and opened the trunk. We all scrambled for our bags.

We didn't have too much closet space. In order to hang our dresses up neatly, we had to hang some of them behind our bedroom door. There was a large, long nail, and it worked out very nicely. We left our shoes in the boxes, labeled with our names, and stored them at the bottom of the closet. We placed our sweaters, underwear, and socks in our dresser drawers. Everything looked so nice and neat. However, by the end of the week, the drawers had to be straightened out.

It was fall, and school had already started. My cousins and I were all used to the school, but it was the first year for Anthony, Louis's son. He was a very kind and helpful person. He joined the Boy Scouts and was very active. He made many friends. Farming was not his favorite work, but he finally learned from my cousins Rocky and Charlie. He became adjusted to his new life.

In the following year Uncle Louis made a significant change. He started to become very controlling over everything to do with the farm and the home. One day when I came home from school, he was sitting by the kitchen table drinking a glass of wine. I just put my books down and removed my coat, and he blurted out, "I think you should quit school and get a job." I mentioned this to my brother Tony, and he told Uncle Louis, "As long as I am working, she will remain in school until she graduates." There was never another word said about it. However, it didn't stop there. There was a photo of me with my brothers on a small round table. He wanted it removed. He would often call me "Queen Elizabeth" because I always liked to have our home kept neat. Many times after I scrubbed the kitchen and dining room floors, he would come in with his shoes soiled from working on the farm, and he refused to remove them or use the rug. I knew he was doing it spitefully. I didn't complain to my aunt, as I didn't want to upset her. His favorite remark to my aunt was "You're always sick, but you never die." He often said it in Italian.

This life with Uncle Louis lasted for many years until his death. He died from a massive heart attack while eating his dinner on a Palm Sunday. He was buried in Connecticut with his first wife. His body was escorted to the Poughkeepsie Bridge by the Marlboro Police, and the hearse and his two sons and a daughter from Connecticut followed the hearse to the cemetery, where he joined their mother and his previous wife. That was the end of Uncle Louis!

My Brothers

Tony

O N December 7, 1941, Japan attacked Pearl Harbor. It was a sneak attack, and we lost many sailors and ships.

I remember this event as if it happened yesterday. It was a Sunday evening, and I was returning from Schlesinger's Bakery on Western Avenue. It was located at the same spot our local bakery is now. Every Sunday I would go to the bakery between 6:00 and 7:00 p.m. to buy the leftover donuts and other pastries at a reduced price. I usually went home with a very large bag or bags full of those goodies.

On my way home from the bakery that evening, as I walked down the hill toward the farmhouse, I could hear loud voices coming from inside. I could also hear the radio on full blast. I couldn't imagine what was going on. As I entered the house, my cousin Kate shouted, "We are at war with the Japs, and they bombed Pearl Harbor!"

In 1942 we were at war with Germany. My brother Tony and Tom Polizzi, also from town, were the first from Marlboro to be drafted. Tony was given a going-away party by Joe DallVechia at Mannese's Restaurant in Milton. There was emptiness in my life when he left. He had been my security. He had always been there to protect me. I prayed very hard for his safety and for the safety of all our troops. I went to the post office every day in the morning, as I knew that was when the mail was sorted. I knew by his return address that he was in training, and that would have to be completed before he was sent overseas. He was with Company I, 117th Infantry. He went overseas in February 1944.

One morning I saw an army car coming down the hill to the farmhouse. My heart dropped. I feared the worst because I had heard that if a death occurred, the military would make a house call to inform the family. A man dressed in uniform got out the car and came to the door. I opened it with my heart pounding and my hands shaking. He had a very serious look on his face, and he spoke with a strong voice. "I am Lieutenant John Harris from the US Army . . . Is this the Pascale residence?" My voice was almost a whisper when I said yes.

The lieutenant continued, "I want to inform you that Sergeant Anthony Pascale has been wounded in Holland, and he is in an American hospital in Germany recuperating. He injured his feet. He was awarded the Purple Heart." My aunt got very emotional when she heard the news but gave thanks to the Lord that he was going to be all right.

After Sergeant Pascale was released from the hospital, he was put back on the front lines. He fought many battles and campaigns. While fighting in the Battle of the Bulge, he discovered a group of soldiers dressed in American uniforms setting up machine guns to the extreme left of the battlefield. He became suspicious because he knew that his troop should be holding the left flank. He climbed over the stone wall to investigate. He called out to the GIs and didn't like the response he received. Tony commanded his troop to open fire on these men and thus saved his platoon and himself because they were German soldiers dressed in American uniforms. Five German soldiers were killed, and the rest were captured. My brother was awarded the Silver Star for gallantry by Major General Leland Hobbs of the Thirtieth Infantry Division. Another time, a Southern soldier under his command was to be sent to the front line. The soldier was terrified of going to the front line and was so distraught. My brother told him that he would change places with him, and the man would be allowed to stay to the rear of the battle. The soldier was so thankful and very much relieved. But a bomb was dropped on the rear of the troops that day, and the soldier perished. My brother would have been killed if he hadn't had the courage to switch places. It was just fate. He kept a picture of St. Anthony on the inside of his helmet throughout his entire campaign.

Knowing my brother Tony as I do, I wasn't surprised by his gallantry. He was always a strong and tough individual. He made sure all his siblings walked a straight line as we were growing up, and we had no regrets there, as it made us better people. When the war was over, we were notified that he would be arriving home on June 29, 1945. He was the first to leave the household and the first to come home. Thank God.

We were all so excited upon his return. It was ten o'clock in the morning when we saw this young man dressed in his army uniform carrying his duffel bag down the hill and over the bridge to the farmhouse. We all ran up to meet him. Only we younger girls were left, as the older girls were married and the other boys hadn't returned home from their military bases. We met him by the bridge and hugged him. The first thing he said to me was, "Is that you, Annie?" It had been three years since he left. I wasn't that skinny girl that he'd left behind. I was nineteen and had just graduated from high school the year before. He was shocked by the changes in all of us. My aunt prepared his favorite dinner, but it was a late meal because all the neighbors stopped by to say hello and welcome him back home. We girls had set the table early that morning with a beautiful white linen tablecloth. To be patriotic we used red and blue dinner napkins, and in the center was a red, white, and blue floral piece. We borrowed the record "When Johnnie Comes Marching Home." It was very appropriate.

Tony had to unwind and shower, as it had been a long trip home. When he finally got settled, we all sat down to a delicious lasagna dinner with delicious meatballs, sausage, and my aunt's favorite green salad. My aunt said her favorite Italian blessing and thanked the Lord for her nephew's safe return.

JOHN

It wasn't much longer after my brother Tony was drafted that my brother John was called to serve his country. He left in February 1943 with two other local residents, Thomas J. Amodeo and Minton Mattice. Sadly, Minton Mattice was killed in Mount Cassino in Italy.

John fought in the battles of Normandy, the Rhineland, and northern France. He belonged to the Sixtieth Engineer Battalion. His service ended on December 20, 1945. On his return he was employed by the Shell Oil Company in Milton. Later, he worked for Local 137 and at times as a barber.

CARMEN

The youngest of the Pascale brothers was Carmen (Mino.) He was very handsome and had a million-dollar smile. He loved sports and also enjoyed traveling. He always drove and never flew. He would often say that if God had wanted him to fly, He would have given him wings.

He left for the army on August 29, 1942, and was discharged on August 29, 1945. The first place that he was stationed was Fort Bragg in North Carolina. A friend of the family also had a brother stationed there, Anthony Colurciello. One day, Anthony's sisters, Emily and Julia, and Grace Pitkins and their friends and I took a Greyhound bus to visit them in Fort Bragg. The other girls were much older than I. I got permission from the principal to make this long trip. We spent three days there, meeting the boys at the end of each day to spend time with them. My brother seemed homesick. The day I left and said good-bye, I was devastated because I had to leave him. Truthfully, I cried from North Carolina to Washington, DC. I was very heartbroken.

On this trip it bothered me that the black people had to sit in the back of the bus, were not able to use the same bathrooms, and were not served at restaurants. I thought that was very cruel. I mentioned to the girls that we are all God's people. That wasn't the end. Once we got to Fayetteville where Fort Bragg is located, we noticed that if the blacks saw white people coming down the sidewalk, the blacks had to cross the street and walk on the other side. Thank God that's not the case anymore.

My brother Carmen departed for overseas in February 1943. He belonged to Company B, Thirty-Fourth Tank Battalion. He was tank commander. He fought in central Europe, Normandy, northern France, Rhineland, and Sicily. He received the Purple Heart when he was blown from his tank.

Once, he and my brother Tony had a visit overseas. Tony had heard that his brother's troop was in the area, and Carmen had actually spotted a vehicle from Tony's outfit. Carmen was taking a shower when a knock came, and in walked Tony. They enjoyed their visit and planned to see each other the next day. When Tony returned to the area, he discovered that Carmen's troop had left.

I am very proud of the Pascale boys for their service to their country during World War II. I thank God for their return home. There were still three more boys in our household who served their country. Rocky, my cousin, was a marine. He volunteered and chose that part of the service. He joined on September 15, 1942, and fought in the battles of Tarawa (the Bloody Battle) and Okinawa. He came home in March 1945.

Charles Carofano was drafted into the army. He spent most of his time in Italy. He was discharged in September 1944.

Anthony Buccieri, Louis's son, joined the Navy. All the boys who lived in my aunt's farmhouse served, and Anthony made the sixth serviceman.

John Pascale

Carmen Pascale

Sgt. Anthony Pascale receiving the Silver Star for gallantry in Germany

LOVE AT FIRST SIGHT

THE BOYS WERE ALSO AWAY when I graduated high school with the class of 1944. I was active in high school. I was a cheerleader for the basketball team, the president of the junior class, and a representative on the student council. We had socials, and I served many times on the committee. We would dance in the large gym to the popular slow and fast dances. A few teachers and sometimes parents would chaperone. The Christmas social was held a week before Christmas. The gym would be decorated with a large tree in the corner, which was trimmed in large colorful lights and many gold, silver, and red bows. A large star on the top of the tree also lit up. Parents made all types of Christmas cookies topped with red sprinkles. The cookies and hot chocolate were served in the cafeteria.

Once you became a sophomore, the big dance was the sophomore hop. The junior prom and the senior ball were the big dances for the other classes. My date for the junior prom was Bruno Ronkese. The prom was well attended, and it was a great evening. After the prom was over, a group of us went to a popular place in New Paltz. I don't remember who drove us, but the other couple with us was Connie Mandrino and Charles Clancey.

I mentioned that Thomas J. Amodeo left for service at the same time my brother John did. I'd had a crush on him since I was fourteen years old. In 1935 he, his mom, Ann, and the rest of the siblings had left Italy for the United States, to make a new life. Their dad, Antonio Amodeo, was already in the United States, and the family was seeking the American dream. Antonio operated a shirt factory on Mott Street in New York. After arriving on his own, he would send money to his wife,

Gaetana, in Italy, and he made many trips to Italy to visit his family. He was living in Milton and working as a shoemaker when he sent for his wife and their five children. The home that he had purchased was completely furnished, and his shoe repair shop was located on Main Street in Milton (today that shoe repair shop is a thriving salon and spa—"The Studio at Stephanie's"). Everything was ready for the family to move in.

Years prior, when World War I broke out, he had been a single man living in the United States and fought in the American army. Now, since he was an American veteran, his wife and children were automatically US citizens. When they arrived here, they all attended the Milton School. Tom was ten years old and couldn't speak a word of English, and his siblings were in the same situation. He told me, after we got friendly, that Miss Dickerson, from the Milton School, would keep them after school to teach them English.

I got to know Tom when his family moved to Marlboro. His father bought the property on 9W across from the old Marlboro Library. Tom started playing baseball with the local boys, and I attended the games to see this handsome teenager pitch—and what a pitcher he was. He was very shy and never said too much, but I never gave up being friendly. In the summer many city people would come to Marlboro for vacations. We had a few places that were popular to the summer visitors. There was one on Lattintown Road operated by the Chillura family. There was also Villa Fontaine and Trecaroco's on South Road. One Saturday night, my brother Carmen and a few of the baseball players were going to the Saturday night dance at Trecaroco's Boarding House, and they invited me to go along. When we arrived, I saw that Tom was there, and he asked me to dance. I was ecstatic. I hadn't believed that this would ever happen to me. We discussed baseball. He said the local team had a game in Westchester, and he was looking forward to pitching that game. Going forward, we still didn't see too much of each other unless we met in town, and then we would say "hi" to each other and say a few words about the team. I was only fifteen at that time and wasn't allowed to meet the girls and boys at Fromel's ice cream parlor or, worse, to go out alone for a walk. My brother Tony was very strict. So Tom and I never really spent time together. It was in February 1942 that Tom was drafted. We never had a commitment. But I did receive some friendly letters, and I never gave up on him as the one I wanted to spend my life with. As I write this, I picture him in his blue sweatshirt covering his broad shoulders, his black wavy hair, and the most beautiful green eyes. Yes, he was the man I wanted to marry.

He spent much of the time fighting battles in Germany, France, and Italy. He fought in the infantry. During one battle in Germany, the weather was below zero, and it was a fierce fight. The Germans were using their machine guns while he and many of his comrades were in foxholes. He said the fighting was very heavy. When the battle was over, he was admitted to the hospital with frozen feet. After his recovery, he was transferred to a military police company and then to the medics.

Graduation

As I mentioned before, my brothers were all in the service fighting for our freedom when I graduated from high school with the class of 1944. I was very sad that my brothers were not present, and I missed my parents very much on this special day. I thought of how proud they would have been to see me in my white cap and gown with the burgundy tassel hanging.

There were forty students in my graduating class. We had a few rehearsals the week before graduation. At one of the rehearsals we marched to "Pomp and Circumstance," played by the band. I felt so much pride that day. I couldn't believe that I was graduating high school and about to start a new life for myself.

Then finally that night was here at last. The chairs in the gym were neatly arranged. That spring the walls of the gym had been painted in a light yellow. A shiny sealer had just been applied to the floor. The windows were also cleaned so that we could see the trees with their beautiful leaves moving in the breeze. A new curtain had been installed on the stage. It was made of very heavy dark green velvet and had a large orange "M" in the center. In front of the stage curtain were baskets of beautiful flowers in bright colors. There was also a basket of flowers in front of the podium. Seated on the stage were the members of the Board of Education—Edward McGowan, president; C. E. Staples; Allen H. Purdy; W. L. Wardell; and Joseph DallVechia. The principal was Edward L. Dalby.

The auditorium was filled to capacity. We were instructed to meet in the cafeteria, where the tables had been removed in order to make room for the graduates. Our caps and gowns were handed out to us, and the girls got busy bobby-pinning the mortar boards so that they were secure on our heads. We there then lined up, according to our height, from shortest to tallest. I was five feet seven inches, which placed me in the third row of our graduation photo and while standing on the stage.

We got the nod to start to proceed in as the band played "Pomp and Circumstance." All in attendance stood up as we entered the gym. My aunt and sisters Mary and Millie were present. Mary had taken a bus from Long Island to be there to honor me. We made our way through the gymnasium and up a short flight of steps and onto the stage. We took our places and stood up until the applause ended. We then said the "Pledge of Allegiance" and took our seats.

Mr. Dalby, our principal, said a few words and then went on with the program. He introduced Marty Bond as the valedictorian, and she spoke on how to be successful in life.

Then it came time to hand out awards. I felt that I would not be eligible for any, but I was happy for those whose names were being called. I was distracted for a minute or so when they called my name and wasn't sure I'd heard right until Mary Dragotta nudged me. I was very happy to hear the applause. The award was written on a long white envelope and read, "P.E.O. Award given to the girl who has shown the greatest improvement in Character and general all around during the 4 years of high school. $10.00 won by Anna Pascale."

At that time $10 was a great award to receive. There were not as many awards given out in 1944 as there are today. For some reason I still have the award envelope with my diploma and my tassel. I must say the envelope is no longer white or new; it is rather a yellowish color and is coming apart. It's almost sixty-seven years old.

As the ceremony ended, we filed out in very orderly fashion down the short flight of steps and back down the aisle to the cafeteria. We all stood neatly in a row to receive congratulations, gifts, and flowers.

I did receive a basket of beautiful flowers from Joseph and Julia DallVechia and monetary gifts from my two elementary teachers, Miss Dowd and Miss Bewick. After the graduation ceremony, we went home. My aunt made a beautiful cake topped with whipped cream and delicious fresh strawberries that had been picked on her farm. The cake seemed very high because in the middle of the two layers there were so many strawberries and whipped cream. The next day my sister Mary left for her home on Long Island. She had enjoyed being together with Millie, Josephine, Anne, and me.

Anne Pascale Amodeo, graduation photo

I already knew what I would be doing after graduation. Six weeks before graduation, Mr. Dalby had informed the senior girls that a position would be opened to a senior to work with the FBI in Washington, DC. Eleven girls who were interested were interviewed in the principal's office.

I do remember this tall handsome FBI agent interviewing me. He asked about members of my family. I told him that I had three brothers fighting in the war. It was 1944, and we were still at war. He asked many questions, and one, I remember vividly. "Were there any murderers in your family?"

I hesitated and said a quick "no." After the interview he shook my hand, and I left the office and went back to class. I was bothered by the question that he had asked. After much thought I felt that I had answered the question correctly. My stepfather was not a blood relative. I felt he was not a member of my family. I felt that I had answered the question honestly. How could I explain to this handsome FBI agent that he was my stepfather? I was too embarrassed to explain it to him. My father was Michael Pascale, not Phillip Deciano.

The following day, I met Father Hanley at the post office, and he said that an FBI agent had stopped at the rectory also to investigate me for the job and had asked the same question about any murders in the family. He told the agent about my stepfather and told him that I was from a good family. Father Hanley explained that my parents had died in their thirties, and my aunt had raised my siblings and me.

The following week, I received a letter from the office of the FBI in Washington, DC, signed by J. Edgar Hoover, Director of the FBI. I was overwhelmed and nervous at the same time upon receiving this appointment. It was a great honor. It was time to move on. I had never left the farmhouse for any kind of vacation. Marlboro and the surrounding communities were the only places I'd ever known.

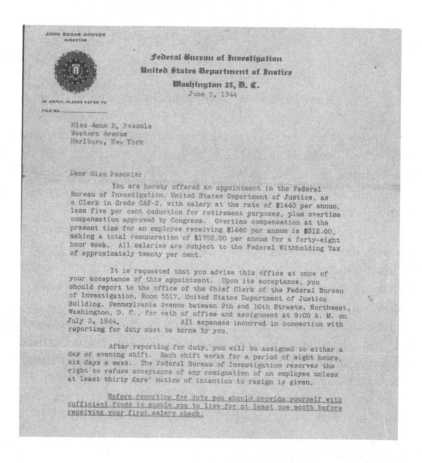

Miss Anna M. Pascale
Marlboro, New York   - 2 -   June 5, 1944

        If you are now or have been essentially employed within
the past sixty days, this appointment is null and void unless you
submit a statement of availability from such employer at the time
you report for duty containing the following information.

        1. Name and Social Security Number, if any.
        2. Name and address of employer.
        3. A statement to the effect that you may be
           hired elsewhere in essential industry.

        The above statement should be dated as of the day of
execution.

        This letter, which should be considered strictly confi-
dential and given no publicity, should be presented when you report
for duty. At the time of reporting for duty, evidence to verify the
correct date of your birth should be furnished.

        For your information, upon arrival in Washington all appointees
are required to submit to a chest x-ray, the expenses of which are to be
borne by the Government.

        Advise by wire collect of your acceptance or declination of
this appointment. If you do not report for duty by the aforementioned
date, the appointment will be cancelled.

                            Sincerely yours,

                            J. E. Hoover
                            John Edgar Hoover
                            Director

The letter I received confirming my appointment by the FBI

I had to leave in the middle of July, which didn't give me much
time after graduation to get some extra clothing and other necessities.
I was fortunate to receive some beautiful cards wishing me well in
my new endeavor. My family and friends were very generous in their
monetary gifts. The letter indicated that I should bring enough money
to last until I received my first paycheck. Mr. Dalby gave some advice.
He wanted me to enroll in extra classes in the evenings. I remember
borrowing a suitcase from Rose Carofano Motisi. I told her as soon as
I could afford to buy my own, I would return it.

The night before my departure, I packed my clothes neatly in the
suitcase. I also took an iron that had been packed away in my aunt's
storage room. It had belonged to my mom. It was very heavy, but I

cherished it, knowing that my mom had once used it and that her hands had been on it.

As I packed it, I could visualize her ironing in that one spot in the kitchen. For that moment I was taken back in time to when I was eight years old, living in the upstairs apartment of the big farmhouse. I realized that I had more packing to do and got out of living in the past. Everything was ready to go in the morning.

I must say, when I left the farmhouse and said good-bye to my aunt and cousins, I felt a mixture of joy and sadness. Mr. Festa took my sister Millie and me to Beacon, where we caught the train to Grand Central. From there we went to Penn Station, where our sister Mary was waiting for us. She was living in Long Island, and she met us there to say good-bye and wish me well before I moved on to Washington, DC.

We had time for some lunch, so we ordered a sandwich of ham, cheese, lettuce, tomato, and mayo and a cold Coke. I felt my throat starting to close up. I just couldn't eat. So I reminded myself, *You have an opportunity of a lifetime.* I then picked up my sandwich and enjoyed every bit of it, and the cold Coke really hit the spot. After lunch we went to the ladies' room and washed our hands. I combed my hair again and applied a light cover of makeup on my face. We then went on the platform, with about ten minutes left before the train was to leave. They told me to be careful and to call when I arrived.

My acceptance letter had said that I would be picked up at the train station in Washington by an FBI agent. Since Washington was overcrowded, a girl named Betty Johnson from Newburgh and I would share an apartment in Arlington, Virginia. We were driven there by the agent. He carted our suitcases in his car, took us directly to the apartment, and unloaded our suitcases.

We were told that we would meet the following day in Room 107 for orientation. The agent showed us the location of the bus stop where we would catch the bus to Pennsylvania Avenue.

The following morning, after a good night's rest, we got up and showered. We dressed very conservatively, put on some light makeup, and gave very little time to our hair since it had held quite neatly after our good "set" from home.

Since Betty and I had done no grocery shopping to fill our small pantry and refrigerator, we stopped at the coffee shop on the corner for a good cup of coffee and a bagel before we boarded the bus. We decided to go grocery shopping after our orientation was over. We had about a five-minute wait before we saw a bus coming. Much to our surprise, it did not stop, as it was filled to capacity. In about seven minutes another bus came and stopped. We took the last two seats.

We got food at the corner of the FBI building and then entered the lobby and showed our IDs to the guard, who gave us directions to Room 107. The medium-sized room was full. An agent explained to us the type of work we would be doing. It had to do with all the servicemen in the US military. After our briefing, we were given a tour of the large building. One memory that remains with me is of the large glass showcase containing a large photo of Al Capone. It also contained the clothes he had been wearing on the day he was captured and the gun he had been carrying. Al Capone was the head of the Chicago crime family. He was very smooth in his dealings, and it had been very hard to convict him on any of his crimes for lack of evidence. He was finally charged with tax evasion.

It was late in the afternoon when our orientation came to an end. Betty and I had dinner in Washington before heading to our apartment in Arlington. Afterward, we boarded the bus again to return home. The bus driver made a complete stop at the corner of our street, and we walked the rest of the way to our building. We walked through the lobby and up a short flight of stairs to our second floor apartment. We entered our small kitchen by passing through the neatly furnished living room and then through our medium-sized bedroom. The bedroom had two twin beds, a small closet, a good-sized dresser, and two windows. In between the twin beds there was a small round table covered with a white lace doily and a pink lamp to match the bedspread and the window curtains. All the floors were covered with linoleum. After a short rest we decided to go to a small grocery store to pick up some items. The small refrigerator was completely empty, and the freezer contained only some ice cube trays filled with ice.

The next morning, it was finally time for us to report for work. We got up early that morning to shower and dress accordingly. Because of the excitement of starting our first day of work, we each had only a glass of juice, coffee, and a slice of toast.

We went down the stairs, exited the building, and walked to the corner bus stop. We both checked to make sure we had our ID cards with us. The first bus again passed us by. We were able to board the next bus. We walked from the bus stop to the FBI building. As we entered, we had our ID cards ready. We proceeded to an enormous room where one of the FBI guards had a sheet of paper listing all of our names. He checked our names and gave us the numbers of our seats. Betty and I were separated.

Against the walls all around this enormous room were files, from the floor to a high spot. Stools were used when necessary to reach the higher files. We were warned again about the confidentiality of these files. At the end of the day, we never spoke about the work we had done. I must say I loved the job very much. It was so different from Marlboro and what my life was like. Of course, after graduation I had never worked in any other kind of job because I had left for Washington after only two weeks.

On our first weekend Betty and I decided to take in some sightseeing. We visited the Capitol, the Lincoln Memorial, and other government buildings. The following day was Sunday, and we attended mass in Arlington. We slept in a bit longer and decided we would go for a healthy breakfast after mass. The mass was packed with many servicemen. The homily was very interesting. The focal point was the war, and the priest encouraged those in attendance to pray for peace. D-day was just over, and we had lost so many soldiers, and the priest was trying to convey—and he did so very successfully—that powerful prayers were needed to end this terrible war.

After mass we took in a healthy breakfast. We enjoyed orange juice, coffee, bacon and eggs, and toast. We then went for a walk in the park. It was very crowded there. We sat under a large beautiful maple tree, and an occasional breeze that ruffled the leaves of the tree relieved the summer heat. There were many baby carriages, several small children running around, and of course, many servicemen. I was hoping that one of the servicemen was one of my brothers. Of course, I knew this was impossible because they had all been deployed overseas. As I sat on the bench, I wondered how my life could change so much, from one of living on a farm in upstate New York to one of working for the FBI in Washington, DC, and living over the bridge in Arlington.

Betty and I finally decide to get an apartment in Washington, DC. We wanted to be closer to our job, and one of the girls told us one day that she had seen an apartment for rent, and there wouldn't be a problem with the bus schedule. That day we worked overtime. We had the phone and address for this new apartment, so we called the number, and the gentleman who answered said that he would be very happy to show us the apartment at eight o'clock that evening. When we were done with our overtime shift, we grabbed a fast sandwich and took a bus to the address. It was a short ride from our workplace.

We got off the bus just a few yards from the apartment. We rang the bell, and the gentleman answered promptly. He said that he'd been expecting us and immediately showed us through the apartment. It consisted of a very small kitchen with a small sink and refrigerator. There was a small hot plate sitting on the counter. The bedroom was of medium size and had two small beds, and there was also a sitting room. We decided to take it. We gave him a small deposit and told him that we would move in on the first of the month, which was only a few days away. We then left the apartment, took the bus to Pennsylvania Avenue, and then caught the bus back to Arlington. It had been a very hectic day. Because we had worked overtime and then gone to view the apartment, it was now ten o'clock in the evening.

Before taking the bus the next morning to work, we notified our landlord that we would be leaving the apartment. We told him the new apartment was more convenient for us because it was closer to our work. As we were riding into work, I suggested to Betty that we should take a bus ride over to our new apartment during lunch to see what the neighborhood looked like during the daytime. We really hadn't seen the neighborhood since we had gone at night, and the neighborhood was dark. We also wanted to check out some of the eating places. We found that there were no decent places to eat except this small hole in the wall. (We went there one night after moving. It was the last time we walked in there. The hamburger and French fries we ordered seemed to be soaked in grease.)

We were very disappointed in the area and realized we'd made a big mistake in leaving Arlington. But since we had given our notice to the previous landlord, we decided that we would have to make the best of it. For the most part, we would near the office before taking the bus back to our new apartment. We would also get some Campbell's Chicken Noodle Soup and buy cold cuts to have in between. Finally, we decided to use our hot plate and refrigerator. It was too expensive to eat out every night. I guess what attracted us to the apartment was that the rent was cheaper, but it turned out that all in all, it was more expensive to live there. Sometimes we would take a taxi home if we worked overtime and had a late dinner. We didn't like to wait at the bus stop for a bus once it turned dark.

Yes, it was a big mistake to leave Arlington. I know I learned a lesson not to rush into things before checking out every aspect.

Coming Home

THREE MONTHS INTO THIS JOB that I loved, I felt something was wrong with me. I started to lose weight. In fact, I lost seven pounds in one month. The feelings from my younger dark days seemed to be coming back. I was reliving the death of my mom and reliving the night my uncle Pete was shot by my stepfather, Phillip.

I desperately needed help. My manager gave me the name of a good doctor and then decided to call and make the appointment for me. She also took the time to take me to the appointment. She made it for one o'clock so she could take me on her lunch hour.

After I spoke to the doctor, he said that I was in a very deep depression. He gave me some pills to take and wanted to see me back in three days. The three days came and went, but there was no improvement. Having been told to take a week of medical leave, I slept most of the day. I had no appetite. I missed my aunt and sister Millie. The doctor felt the surroundings of my home might help me. I felt it was the dark days of my childhood that had brought on this illness.

I realized that staying at the apartment alone was no help. The doctor told me the progress I was making was very slow and that the medication I was on should have had better results. I took the doctor's advice and sought permission to leave my job. During the war, your job was frozen, and you had to get a release. I had no problem getting released, and at the same time it was one of the sad things I had to do. I knew that I wasn't getting completely well. Some days were better than others. I knew I couldn't perform my job to the fullest.

I went with Betty one day to say good-bye to the girls and to my manager. My manager understood but had much regret about me leaving. She was very graceful as I handed her the release that the doctor had signed. She felt I was doing a great job and had a good future. The following day, a Saturday, Betty decided to visit her family in Newburgh. She was very kind to me and helped me pack my belongings.

One of the FBI agents picked us up at the apartment as a special favor. The ride going past the FBI building on Pennsylvania Avenue made me feel very sad. The area was so crowded, and the traffic was busy with cars and buses.

We finally arrived at the train station. The kind agent got out, opened our door, and removed our suitcases from the trunk of the car, and a porter brought the luggage into the station. The agent shook my hand and wished me a full recovery. What followed felt like the longest train ride I'd ever had. I must say I was devastated, but I knew it was no fault of my own.

I got tired from the medications when I was on the train but managed to stay awake. I knew my sisters Mary and Millie would be at Penn Station to meet me. As the train came to a halt, I looked out of the window, and there were my two sisters. Betty helped me out with my luggage. As I came off the train, my sisters greeted me with hugs and kisses. They realized that I didn't look too well, but with some good food I would be well real soon. My sister Mary took the Long Island train to Jamaica. Millie, Betty, and I took the Trailway bus up to Newburgh. Betty's father drove Millie and me to Marlboro, and I said good-bye to Betty and thanked her for all her kindnesses.

Coming into Marlboro down the hill to the farmhouse, I became very confused for a moment, and I told myself that I had to get better. My aunt was very happy to see me. She was a very emotional person, and she immediately cried and hugged me. The first words out of her mouth were "I made delicious chicken soup with homemade noodles." She uncovered the pot to show me, and I saw all kinds of vegetables in the soup. It sure smelled good. It was a sign of how happy she was to see me and that I was home.

Uncle Louis was asleep on the couch. When he woke up, he didn't have much to say. We were never on good terms. My aunt was waiting for the water to boil so she could cook the noodles that she had prepared. Once they were cooked, she drained them and put them in the chicken soup. She then took out the Italian grating cheese and put a thick layer on the top. The smell was unbelievable, but the taste was fantastic. The first week I was home, I made great improvement. My aunt continued to make me healthy meals, and I could feel that I was getting stronger. My energy was starting to return. My girlfriend Gaye Festa came down every day. Anne Goodfriend (Olsen) was a constant visitor too. She lived in one of the apartments owned by Jim Festa. (We were known as the Three Musketeers.)

After three weeks at home, I decided to look for some employment. I loved office work, including payroll. I checked the newspaper and found there were openings at the Bobrich-Debway in Beacon for clerical work. Gaye and I applied and were interviewed. We were both hired, and we started work the following week. The factory was attached to the office. Those who were employed in the factory manufactured electric blankets.

Joe Colletta, a local resident who was employed in the factory, was kind enough to pick us up and drive us to Beacon every day. He would pick us up on Western Avenue and drive directly to the Newburgh-Beacon ferry. It was more convenient than taking the bus, the ferry, and then another bus to the office. The charge for the trip with Joe was $2.50/week.

Meanwhile, the war was still going on. We received a letter from my brother Tony telling us he had met our brother Carmen in Germany. They were very happy to have had this chance meeting, as it was just by coincidence that their battalions were in the same area that day. They spoke about their battles, and they had heard of my illness and were very sad about it; however, they were happy that I had come home and was getting the right care.

Supporting Our Troops

I was finally settled in with my sister Millie and my cousins Josephine, Annie, and Antoinette. The rest of the girls had married and had their own homes, and the six boys were all off serving their country. One day I mentioned to Gaye and Anne Goodfriend that we should be doing something to help our country and our servicemen. But at the time we didn't know what to do.

The following day, as we were coming home from work, we passed a large billboard advertising, in large blue and red letters on a white background, "JOIN THE USO." On the side of the large poster stood a soldier dressed in his army uniform. We got the answer to our question.

Without hesitation I was on the phone getting the information we needed to join the USO in Newburgh. It was affiliated with Stewart Field. With all the information, we went to our first affair in this beautiful building on Grand Street off Broadway.

The first thing the president of our group showed us was the kitchen and how to use the huge coffeepot there. The tables had to be arranged in a certain way for different games. There were records and a record player that were used only for Friday or Saturday night dances. There was always something going on. Most of the activities were held on the second floor.

The first affair for which Gaye, Anne, and I were on the planning committee was an October Fest. We sat down and planned the orange and black tablecloths with matching napkins, candles, colorful leaves, pumpkins, and corn stalks. Most of the latter, we could get from our hometown farmers. The apple cider that we planned to serve was being given to us by Joe DallVechia's Cider Mill. We went to Woolworth's 5 and 10 to purchase decorations, but when we got to the store, the manager told the register clerk that the supplies would be donated by Woolworth's. Of course we were now left with the purchase of the food. We decided on hot dogs and sauerkraut, German potato salad, and a special veal dish that one of the GIs said his mother made; it was baked as a veal cutlet and breaded with special spices, and it was a big hit. The food was enjoyed by all. The meal was served buffet style, and the long table was covered with the orange and black tablecloths. Candles and three carved pumpkins with thick candles inside that gave a beautiful glow were on the table too. The dishes were in fall colors, and the silverware was wrapped in the festive napkins. The dessert was a large German chocolate cake that sat on a separate table. Paper cups were placed at each setting on the table, and in the middle of each table was a beautiful arrangement of fall flowers donated by Velie's Nursery on Old Post Road in Marlboro.

The farmers in Marlboro were so generous that each eating table had a carved-out pumpkin lit with a candle inside. It was a beautiful picture. The corn stalks were placed in each of the corners of the room.

The businesses in Newburgh and Marlboro were generous as well with their donations. The USO was a great place for soldiers to go in their free time. We were getting used to the routine of the activities at Grand Street in Newburgh at the USO Headquarters. We would usually get dropped off by someone else who was making the trip to Newburgh and then would take a taxi home. Since the three of us were steady customers, we were given a special discount.

After attending the USO, you would more or less get friendly with a certain soldier. Every time I went and wasn't on duty, Ted and I would find ourselves together. He was a Polish Catholic soldier from Alpena, Michigan. I enjoyed his company very much. We would play different games or dance.

The very important dances were held at the Officers' Club at Stewart Field. The big-name bands would play there, and it was very formal. We three girls always attended. Some of the bands were Tommy Dorsey, Harry James, and Vaughn Monroe. At one dance we attended, Don Cornell sang many of the songs from Glenn Miller's collection (he was killed in a plane crash). He wrote "White Cliffs of Dover" and "I'll Be Seeing You." With all these beautiful songs being sung, there was always sadness among the joy because our soldiers were being killed, and there was no end to the war in sight.

When I first became a member of the USO, I was just there to help entertain our boys. I had no intention of getting serious with anyone because Tom was the man of my dreams. I knew we weren't committed to each other, but I wasn't giving up. We had been corresponding, and the letters had a friendly tone.

Gaye was dating Lt. Richard Mooney, and Anne Goodfriend was dating LaMar Olsen from Utah. Then there was my friend Ted and I. One Saturday night, we three couples decided to have dinner at the Green Room on Broadway, the popular spot in Newburgh. Before dinner, Lieutenant Mooney presented Gaye with an engagement ring, and much to our surprise, she accepted (after six months, their engagement was broken). Anne Goodfriend eventually married LaMar and settled in Ogden, Utah. He was a Mormon, but Anne kept her Catholic religion, and her children were brought up as Catholics. They were a beautiful family. A few years later, Gaye left Marlboro and moved out west to Ogden, Utah, too. She later met and married Glenn Paulsen. Their son Glenn is a very respectful and caring person. Gaye and Glenn Sr. divorced, and she moved back to Marlboro. She now resides with her brother, Pat Festa.

Back during our USO days, Ted and I began seeing each other more often. He seemed to be getting serious, and I was getting used to being with him and enjoyed his company very much. I always held back because of my feelings for Tom, though. Ted knew this, as I often mentioned it. I must admit it was easy—very easy—to fall in love with him, as he was a gentleman in the full sense of the word. Ted came up with Gaye's friend and Anne's friend to Marlboro sometimes, and Gaye's mother would cook a delicious Sunday dinner. Sometimes they would make it a long weekend, sleeping in Mrs. Festa's attic. Mrs. Festa would have a great breakfast ready on Sunday mornings. I would be there at nine o'clock, in time for breakfast, and Ted and I would attend the eleven o'clock Sunday mass.

I remember one Sunday when 9W wasn't plowed too well and it was icy. Ted and I walked to church. We walked past the Amodeo household, located where the Sunoco garage is now. I was told later that Tom's parent weren't too happy about seeing me walking with another man. Because Tom and I corresponded, they felt Tom and I were committed to each other. Their ideas were from the old country.

After mass, Mrs. Festa set a large oval table in her finished basement that could seat at least twenty people. The table was set for a king and queen and their attendants. It was a complete roast beef dinner, and her dessert was the Butterfly, a large cupcake with vanilla pudding and two wings made of dough placed on each side of the cupcake, with the center filled with whipped cream. It was to die for. Then it was time for our GI friends to leave for their army base at Stewart Field. Mr. Festa drove them back. It sure was a lovely weekend.

Monday came quickly, and we were once again back to work. I had a couple of beautiful surprises. Kitty Doyle, my office manager, called me into the inner office to tell me that I was receiving a promotion along with a substantial raise. She told me that I was very dedicated to my work. Kitty is still living in Beacon at the age of ninety-four.

Later that morning, I received a phone call from Ted. He wanted to take me out for dinner that evening and then go to a movie. I told him to call me back in a half-hour. I told Kitty about the date with Ted and decided not to accept the invitation, as I wasn't dressed for the occasion. She insisted that I borrow money from the petty cash and pay it back when I got my paycheck. I could then go to the dress shop around the corner from my job. I ended up taking her advice. I bought a beautiful black dress with a V-neck. I had happened to wear pearls that day with matching earrings.

Joe, the man who drove Gaye and me to work, left me off by the bank on Broadway, and there was Ted with a smile on his face. I thanked Joe for going out of his way to drop me off. Ted and I crossed Broadway hand in hand. He said that he had made reservations at the Green Room. We had a beautiful table set for two in the corner. On the table was a Waterford vase with the most beautiful red rose. He said to me, "Whenever you use this vase, think of me," and I must say I felt sad. A minute later the piano player announced he had a request for the song "I'll Be Loving You Always." That really put the icing on the cake. Since it was rather early for a crowd to be there for dancing, Ted got up and said he would like to dance to this beautiful song. After the dance, we sat down and ordered a glass of wine. I needed a glass of wine because of what was happening. In a low voice I explained to him that I really didn't want to lead him on, as Tom was always in my thoughts. He understood and told me that Tom was a very lucky guy. I must say that I did have some feelings for him. We both ordered steak that evening. It was a bittersweet evening that I will never forget.

We saw the movie in which the song "It Had to Be You" played. Lauren Bacall and Humphrey Bogart were in it, and what a terrific movie it was. We left the movie, and Ted saw a taxi coming down Broadway and went into the road to stop it. He gave me a short kiss and paid the taxi driver, and in a moment, I was on my way home in the taxi. I must say I felt somewhat uncomfortable after that beautiful evening. I still get the picture of that evening when I hear that song—"It Had to Be You." We continued to see each other at the USO.

THE END OF THE WAR

THE WAR ENDED IN EUROPE in April 1945 and in the Pacific in August 1945. It sure was a celebration. When the European war was over, Gaye and I happened to be clothes shopping. People were shouting on Broadway as cars rode by with their horns blowing. Restaurants were overcrowded, and the jukeboxes were playing war songs, including ones from World War I. Some of the ones I remember were "When Johnnie Comes Marching Home," "White Cliffs of Dover," and "Sentimental Journey." We finally got on the bus for our trip home. Leaving the bus station to go on Water Street was a disaster. Cars were parked anywhere they could find a space. We finally got on Broadway to pick up other passengers who were going to Middle Hope, Marlboro, Highland, and farther north. There was joy in everyone we met. People kept shouting, "It's over!" When I got home, my aunt was full of joy because she knew all her boys were coming home, and in the same moment, she felt sad for the ones who were not coming home.

VJ Day was a little different for me. Gaye, Anne Goodfriend, and I had been invited to visit my cousin Rose Carofano Motisi, who lived in Brooklyn, for a few days. We decided to go to New York City the day that everyone knew the war in the Pacific was over. We were in Times Square and were pushed every way you could think of. You just went with the crowd. At times we got separated. Do you remember the sailor who kissed the nurse on Times Square? That is just what it was like—joy. The excitement was so great that everything was okay that day. We were unable to go into any kind of restaurant for lunch or dinner. We decided to go back to Brooklyn after a rough, happy day. As we walked to the subway stations, we automatically walked into other people, as the sidewalks were so crowded. Some did too much celebrating on the bus. But everything went that day. The policemen ignored a lot even though they did try very hard to keep order.

We finally got on the subway with more people celebrating and got to my cousin's apartment, but not before we found ourselves joining the local neighborhood parties. There were block parties being planned throughout Brooklyn. When we finally got inside my cousin's apartment, she was preparing dinner. In the meantime, her husband Frank was mixing some drinks from red, green, and clear liquids. The bottles were shining and very pretty. I had no experience with drinking alcohol, but I also thought that I should celebrate with a small cordial glass. It tasted good, and I decided to have one of each color. But I was drinking on an empty stomach since we hadn't been able to eat in NYC, and my cousin was still working on preparing dinner. I became so sick. I was unable to eat and also missed out on going to the block dance. My cousin and I still talk about that day. My cousin stood by my side that evening. She was very concerned for me. Gaye and Anne enjoyed the block dance, as they had not drunk the way I had earlier in the evening. They enjoyed dinner as well. I sure learned from that experience. What a day to remember!

My brothers were away for three years serving their country. Much took place while they were away. My cousin Antoinette, who had Down's syndrome, passed away at the age of thirteen. She continued to ask about the boys until the very end.

All the boys who lived in the farmhouse returned from the war. Bottom row (l-r): John Pascale, Vito Valentino (friend), Charles Carofano. Top row (l-r): Carmen Pascale, Rocco Carofano, Anthony Buccieri, Anthony (Tony) Pascale, Mike Cutillo (friend).

Tom's Homecoming

SINCE THE WAR WAS OVER, many of the GIs were being discharged. The days were getting shorter, and the nights were getting longer. The cold winter was upon us, along with the snow. Ted was notified that he would be discharged on December 4, 1945.

I met him at the ferry and accompanied him to Beacon and to the train station. He was headed back to Alpena, Michigan. It was a cold, cloudy day as we waited on the platform. He said that he would write once he got home and settled. From a distance you could hear the sound of the train, and I did feel a void at that moment. Ted gave me a hug and a short kiss good-bye. I saw him get on the train; he was seated by the window. I waited and watched as the train left very slowly, until his beautiful smile faded away.

I left and got on the ferry back to Newburgh to take the bus home. Gaye and Anne came down that evening to keep me company. The next day, I was back to my routine at work. The following Saturday, we went to the USO. But the USO was never the same for me. I never thought that Ted's going home would affect me that way.

After four days I received a beautiful note from Ted. The trip home to Michigan had been rather long. He was happy to see his family. He was going to take a rest before looking for employment. Since he was in the Air Force, he was interested in going to pilot school. I must say I did miss him, but I kept busy preparing for Christmas. We wanted to make it a special Christmas since this was the first time the boys had been home since the war.

On December 20, 1945, much to my surprise, as I was putting a beautiful wreath on our door, I spotted Tom walking down the hill. I ran inside, quickly combed my hair, and added a light cover of makeup. Just as I finished, a knock came at the door. I ran down to answer it and welcomed him in. He seemed much older but was still as handsome as ever. He sat at the kitchen table, and I put on a pot of coffee. My brother John walked in, and they gave each other a hug. They hadn't seen each other since they left Marlboro together in February 1942, when they had been in the same draft. More than three years had passed. They spoke about their war days over a cup of coffee. They didn't yet know that Minton Mattice, the fellow who had left with them, had been killed at Monte Cassino, Italy.

Tom asked me for my phone number as he was leaving and asked if it would be all right to call me. I had no problem with that.

The following day, I received another letter from Ted. He asked me if Tom had gotten home yet. He wanted me to write and give him all the details about Tom coming home. That night Tom called and asked if it would be all right if he came to visit, and I said that would be fine. We couldn't go to a movie or out for dinner, as Tom didn't have a car yet. It sure was nice to be able to spend some time together. Things started to fall into place, and I knew it was Tom who would fill my life with complete happiness.

I wrote Ted late that evening and told him that I was spending quite a bit of time with Tom and still felt like I always had—that he was the one that I was really waiting for. I told Ted I had enjoyed the time I spent with him at the USO and other time we spent together, and I would always cherish the friendship and have the deepest respect for him as a perfect gentleman. Six months later, I heard from him again; he had met a nice girl named Jennifer from Alpena, and they were serious. I was very happy for him and said Jennifer was a lucky girl to have met him. I signed my letter, "May God Bless you both. Anne." When Tom was visiting me one evening, I spoke about Ted to him. I told him that we had met at the USO and enjoyed many evenings together with the rest of the USO gang.

One day Tom called and told me that he would like to take me out for dinner and to a movie. He wondered if we could borrow my brother John's car. I asked, and of course my brother agreed.

We did have an enjoyable evening. We went to Peppy's in Newburgh and had veal marsala and a delicious salad with roasted peppers and olives in a very tasty dressing. I can't forget the side order of spaghetti. On the way home he asked me if I would date only him. I thought to myself, *Is he kidding?* But aloud I said, not too anxiously, "Sure." This was the best thing I'd heard since I was fourteen. The Lord had had a different plan for me when I left Washington with my illness. My dream was coming true. The USO was still active, but I was no longer a member. Gaye and Anne continued their involvement and enjoyed it. I felt the war was over, and I had contributed many hours in bringing joy to our servicemen from Stewart Field. I'd devoted much time to planning parties and dances and serving coffee and desserts. At this time, I wanted to devote my time to my job and to Tom.

Tom and I when we were courting (1946)

My brother John was employed by Union Local 137 Engineers. At the time, the local was hiring, and my brother told Tom about it. Tom got a job operating different equipment. He worked on many IBM buildings and on the construction of roads. He later got his union book, which gave him medical benefits and a pension. Then he became a part-time police officer for the town of Marlboro. Still later, he became part-owner of the Sunoco station with his brother John. His construction job was his main job, and he divided some weekends and evenings with the police department and the gas station. His income from his other two jobs was pooled in the gas station. It worked very well with Tom and John. I didn't see too much of Tom except every other Sunday or every other evening, when it wasn't his turn to work at the gas station. John had more time to spend with his girlfriend, Fannie Porpiglia. Tom finally bought a car, which he and his brother John shared. It worked out well because when one was working, the other had the evening off.

At this time the farmhouse was busy, with the boys home from service. They often invited their friends to come and chat or play a game of horseshoes. It wasn't long before my cousin Rocky opened a pizza place. My aunt bought the property up on Western Avenue. There was a house there where Lizzie Williams, the housekeeper for Father Hanley, lived. Rocky had a pizza oven put down in the basement and sold pizzas in the evening. My aunt had a new road built to the farmhouse. The road going on Festas' property was then closed, and a new bridge was built to go over the brook. Rocky's pizza business was terrific. The price of a pizza was $1.25. If you added a topping of mushrooms, pepperoni, or peppers, the pizza cost $1.50.

The house was then repaired, and after Rocky's marriage to Lena Roselli and his brother Charlie's marriage to Mary Gerentine, the brothers decided to put up a building and continue with the pizzas, dinners, and a bar business. It went very well for many years. It was called the 4Cs, after the four Carofanos.

The Engagement

It was Christmas of 1946, and Tom had been out of the service for a year already. We'd had a beautiful year together, and our love grew stronger as the days went by. Tom worked very hard. Christmas of 1946 was one of my happiest. We got engaged. I knew about the event in advance. I quickly went to a jewelry store in Beacon where I worked and bought him a beautiful black onyx ring with a diamond chip in a fourteen-karat gold setting. Back in 1946, a $75 ring was considered a good-quality ring. I put down a $25 deposit and paid $10 a week for the next five weeks.

We decided to get engaged on Christmas Eve before the Midnight Mass. Tom's mother Gaetana had brought with her from Monteforte, Italy, a tradition of celebrating Christmas Eve with a special fish dinner. We started at six o'clock, and the feast lasted for hours. She prepared just about every kind of fish. Some were baked or fried. Some of the fish was used to make a white sauce that was poured over spaghetti. My favorite fish was lobster tails or breaded fried shrimp. The lobster tail was baked and then placed under the broiler. It sure was a picture with the melted butter and golden look. The shrimp was dipped in a spicy egg wash and then in a flavored bread crumb with the aroma of garlic. The oil in the frying pan was ready for its victims. After the frying, the shrimp were removed and placed on a paper towel to absorb the extra oil. Gaetana finally placed them on a round platter, with lemon wedges surrounding the beautiful creatures. They were always a hit. There were also tiny fish covered with olive oil, oregano, and garlic and baked on a cookie sheet. Tom's parents enjoyed them, but I wouldn't have them anywhere near me. They upset my stomach. The spaghetti was always a big hit as well.

This delicious dinner was always served with a white wine. Tom's father knew his wines and always chose the right one to go with the meals his wife prepared. He always said a meal without wine was like a day without the sun. He would then add that water makes your pipes rusty.

We had some light dessert after this hardy and delicious fish dinner. The grapes were appealing to me because they were sweet and cold and refreshing. We sat around and chatted about Christmas Eve in Italy. Tom's mother was an excellent cook. Any food she prepared had so many flavors, especially her meatballs. She was a very kind and gentle person.

I took a look at my watch and realized Tom and I had to get ready for the Midnight Mass. We wanted to leave and arrive at the church early because we were going to get engaged. We wanted to be there at eleven o'clock to have some privacy.

Tom's father made a special toast on the engagement that was going to take place. It went something like this: "May our Lord give you both the joy and happiness you are sharing at this moment for many years to come."

We left for church, and I felt like I had a new beginning in life. Tom parked the car, and we walked up the stairs to the front door. We entered the church and blessed ourselves as we looked down the middle aisle and saw the sanctuary's white marble altar, where white candles held by gold candle holders sent out a beautiful glow. Red poinsettias were displayed in shiny gold foil pots. The tabernacle door, where our Lord presented the holy wafers, was so radiant with its golden front. On either side of the altar there stood a beautiful marble angel. Yes, we realized it was a special holy night for the birth of our Savior. After standing there for a moment, we went down the left aisle, where the statue of the Sacred Heart stood on a pedestal. A smaller statue of the infant of Prague was to the left on a smaller pedestal.

A candle rack was in front with red and blue glass candle holders. Tom and I each lit a candle and kneeled and said a silent prayer. Tom then held my hand and placed a beautiful one-carat diamond ring with a platinum band on my finger. He said, "I love you." In return I took his hand and placed the black onyx ring on his finger and said in a soft tone, "I love you and will always".

As we stood there, I raised my eyes to our Blessed Mother, behind the Sacred Heart and the statue of Prague. On her beautiful altar she was looking down upon us. I said thank you to my Heavenly Mother and Earthly Mother. It was getting closer to 11:30, and the choir members were starting to enter the church and take their places on the left to begin the Christmas carols before the Midnight Mass started. Tom and I took our seats on the left side. I couldn't help the joy I felt. I was so full of the Holy Spirit that I could have flown home after the mass. I could see from Tom's face that he felt the same way as he squeezed my hand.

As we sat there, I couldn't help but notice how the nativity set was placed on the right side of the sanctuary in front of the beautiful white marble altar with the Statue of St. Joseph. It was so appropriate.

I had never felt the security and love that I felt at that very moment. At 11:30 sharp, Mrs. Downer started the organ on the left side of the altar, which signaled the choir to begin. The choir consisted of about ten members, and Rose Dugan Rusk was the soloist. At twelve o'clock, Father Hanley and the altar boys walked in as the choir sang "Silent Night." It was Tom's favorite Christmas carol. He said it was the first Christmas carol he had heard in St. James Church in Milton on his first Christmas here from Italy. The cross and candle holders were shining. Father Hanley always gave a very meaningful homily, and it was no different this evening. After the mass was over, Tom and I stopped to wish Father Hanley a Merry Christmas, and we told him that we had gotten engaged. He was very happy for me. Father Hanley was very close to my family, and he was always very helpful.

Since it was a mild evening, Tom parked his car in front of his house and walked me home. A full moon shone above, many stars lit the sky, and there was a slight cover of snow on the ground from the two previous days. We stopped on the bridge and could hear the water running beneath us. The mild weather had melted most of the ice. There was a slight breeze, and in the light of the moon and stars, we could see as well as feel our hair moving. As we chatted, Tom put his arms around me very tightly and whispered in a romantic voice that he would like me to be his wife this coming June. I was very happy and surprised. I didn't think it would be that soon after our engagement. In a soft voice I answered that I would love to have him as my husband. I told him how happy he had made me when he came home from the war and wanted me to be his girlfriend. My life had started to change then. I felt love, kindness, compassion, and security with him.

He was a gift sent to me by our Lord and Blessed Mother. I had finally found my prince whom I had thought would never come.

He asked me to pick a date in June. When I went to the office that Monday, I told the girls what had taken place on Christmas Eve. They were so excited for me. Immediately, they all circled around me to see my engagement ring. They all loved the shape and the brilliance. A minute later, they took out the 1947 calendar to check the Sundays in June. (That was when most marriages were performed.) They didn't have to look too long. June 1 was the first Sunday in June. It was perfect, as I didn't want to wait any longer if I didn't have to.

The Day That Changed My Life—Our Wedding

O F COURSE, THERE WAS A lot of planning to do, and with Tom working so many hours, I had the job of getting things rolling. It happened that Tom's parents had an empty apartment in a building where the Sunoco Service Garage is now located. (The building was torn down some years after Tom's parents passed.)

I was very fortunate to have my brother John handy to do some minor carpenter work. There was much to be done in this apartment. Painting, wallpapering, and replacing the kitchen cabinets were on our to-do list. Tom would assist on his Sundays off, which wasn't too often.

Our entrance was from 9W. Across from our apartment was the old Marlboro Free Library, followed by Rusk and Rusk Law Office, Cumiskey's grocery store, and then the First National Bank, which was located on the corner of 9W and King Street.

By the middle of March, the work on the apartment was completed. It turned out to be a very cozy apartment. At that time wallpapering was the way to go. I picked out all the colors and patterns. At the time a red and white kitchen was the style. Red was the accent for my white cabinets, refrigerator, and stove, and there was a touch of red in the curtains that covered the window facing the Hudson River. The kitchen table was white, and the chairs had red plastic seat covers. The white linoleum floor had a red line going through it. The living room was furnished with a small sectional in beige and a light brown sofa with a matching chair. The floor was a flowered beige rug with light orange flowers that gave it life. Of course, the end tables and lamps gave the room a warm and cozy look. The bathroom, located between the living room and bedroom, was a nice size. It had a linoleum floor with a black and white square design. The bathtub was white, as was the sink. The bedroom was the largest room. Our first bedroom was made of dark wood. We purchased the furniture at the Ware House. We stayed within our budget, as we wanted to start our married life without any debt.

The wedding plans were made for Sunday, June 1, at two o'clock at St. Mary's Church on Rte 9W in Marlboro.

My godmother was Carrie Valentino. Her sister worked in a bridal factory in New Jersey and said she would be happy to bring me there to get my wedding gown and veil at a discount. The following Friday, my godmother and I took the train out of Newburgh to Hoboken. We arrived at the house, and her sister greeted us and insisted we have some lunch before going to the factory. It sure was a good lunch and a nice break.

She drove us about four blocks to the factory. I must say I was excited and hoping to find a beautiful gown. As we entered the second floor of the factory and walked into the room, we saw gowns hanging all over the place.

I was very calm as I gently pushed each gown aside as it hung on its hanger. I decided to look at each section of the room where the gowns were hanging. I made sure I didn't miss any one of them. Finally, I went back to the very first group I'd looked at and knew the one I wanted.

The satin gown featured a square neck, long sleeves that were tight at the wrist, a form-fitting waist, five tiers of organdy ruffles from the knees down covered by a very light netting, and two bows. It gracefully touched the top of my shoes, which the sales girl also had me try on. I fell in love with the gown. It was a perfect fit. She had me keep the gown on until we'd found the perfect veil to go with it. Since the gown had a beautiful long train, a fingertip veil was appropriate. The crown of the veil was made of miniature orange blossoms. The price of the gown and veil was half the amount I would have had to pay in a bridal store. It was a great savings.

My husband would have to rent a tuxedo for that special day. Gaye, my maid of honor, bought a beautiful yellow gown with matching head piece. John, Tom's brother, also rented a tuxedo. Last but not least, we rented St. Mary's Hall for our reception. The hall was located on the left side of the church, where part of the parking lot now is. It was a long two-story building. It was used for many church functions as well as parties and weddings.

We had to do one more thing to complete the wedding day: get in touch with a photographer. In those days there were no following photographers who would start to take pictures from the home of the bride. We had to make an appointment with the Galati's photographer. We had to allow time for the wedding ceremony and the receiving line and travel time to Newburgh. We didn't have a limousine. My cousin Josephine's husband, Ossie Gerentine, drove us in his 1947 Buick. Everything was set to go on June 1, 1947.

Tom's brother Bert and his sister Fortuna were in charge of preparing the food, which consisted of different cold cuts on hard and soft rolls, chips, soda, beer, cookies, and a beautiful wedding cake from Café Aurora in Poughkeepsie. The cake had a cannoli filling with whipped cream, and it was delivered at the time the cake was to be cut. The refrigerator in the hall wasn't big enough to hold the cake.

The plans were all made except a tuxedo for my brother Tony. Tony would be walking me down the aisle and giving me away on my wedding day. He left work early on the Friday before the wedding to be fitted.

My sister Mary came from Long Island, and my sister Millie came from North Carolina along with my brother-in-law, Bob.

The day arrived, June 1, 1947. Both of my sisters helped me get dressed that morning. I took the rollers out of my hair and put on my wedding dress. A towel was placed over my shoulders as my hair was brushed out. With no air conditioning I was worried about whether my hair would stay in place. There wasn't any hair spray in 1947. However, it stayed very nicely. The veil was then placed on my head. I realized I didn't have any makeup on. I quickly put on a light cover of powder with a slight dash of rouge for my cheeks and some soft pink lipstick.

I stood up and looked in a long mirror and was satisfied by what I saw. My sister would make sure the train of my gown was pulled out as far as it could be before I walked down the aisle. It was 1:45, which gave me fifteen minutes to make it to the church. I couldn't believe that this special day was here, and in a very short time I would be Mrs. Thomas Amodeo. It sure sounded beautiful to me.

My sisters helped me as I stepped into the waiting car, holding up the train of my gown. They drove to church with me. My brother Tony was already in the front seat with Ossie, the driver. The best man, Tom's brother John, was already at the church. Gaye, my maid of honor, was in the front of my car. Her father had driven her down. She was dressed in a beautiful pale yellow gown and a matching headpiece. She looked beautiful with her long black hair. Gaye's car moved forward, and Ossie pulled up to the center of the sidewalk. He climbed out of the car and helped my two sisters and me out. It was 2:05 when we started to walk up the front step, my two sisters helping to hold up the train. Gaye led the way up the steps to the entrance of the church.

As my brother and I stood at the entrance, I realized that I had been baptized, made my Holy Communion, been confirmed, and now was being married in the same church and by the same priest, Father James Hanley. As we stood there waiting for Mrs. John Downer to play the organ, I could see my prince standing handsomely tall in his tux and his handsome brother standing next to him. The organ started to play, and Gaye started to walk down the aisle. Tony and I followed, and when we arrived in front of the altar, my brother picked up my veil very neatly over my face, kissed me, and gently gave me to Tom. Tom just stared at me with true love in his eyes. We said our marriage vows to each other strongly and sincerely. Father Hanley congratulated us. We turned and walked down the aisle as man and wife. A very happy feeling came over me. Yes, I felt like a princess. I knew I would have a very happy life with my husband.

John and Gaye walked down the aisle behind us. Gaye was so radiant, and John was smiling with happiness. We stood in the receiving line for half an hour. Then we walked out very carefully, holding the train of my gown. Tom opened the back door of Ossie's car, and we both got in very slowly. My brother Tony got in the front seat, and we were on our way to Newburgh to Galati's studio to have our wedding pictures taken. After our pictures were done, Ossie drove us directly to St. Mary's Hall for the reception. The guests were still arriving. We waited on the first floor of the hall until all the guests had arrived and were settled and for Mr. Clark, the piano player who was supplying the music for the evening.

Soon we were told to come up the stairs, as Mr. Clark was ready for us to make our entrance. The first to be announced were my brother Tony and sister Mary. As we entered the room, Gaye and John were announced. Then Mr. Clark announced Mr. and Mrs. Thomas Amodeo and started to play the song, "Let Me Call You Sweetheart," which we had chosen for our first dance. The best man John and his fiancée, Fannie Porpiglia, joined us.

105

It seemed as though all the guest were enjoying themselves. The rolls were filled with delicious cold cuts and were being served with the drinks as well. Many of the guests were dancing fast and slow numbers. Of course my sister Millie danced to the fast numbers. At the midpoint of the reception, the guests started to come and congratulate us and give us monetary gifts.

I remember particularly Julia DallVechia handing us a wedding card and saying to Tom, "You be good to her." He certainly was! It was a wonderful reception enjoyed by all who attended. When it was finally over, Ossie drove me home to remove my gown and get into my going-away suit and then took Tom home to change out of his tux. He waited for Tom and then came to pick me up. Since I'd gotten dressed at my aunt's house, that was where my suitcase was. Ossie and his wife, Josie, drove us to Poughkeepsie, where we would spend the night. We were very thankful to Ossie for driving us that early afternoon and again after the reception. The next morning, we took the train to Niagara Falls.

It was a five-hour trip to Niagara Falls. We had a lot to talk about, including the wedding and what a good time everyone had had at the reception. We arrived at the train station and took a taxi to our hotel. It was located in a very nice area, and it was easy to make connections for the sightseeing tours that were advertised. We stopped in the lobby and got the key to our room. It was beautiful and spacious. The first thing we did was hang our clothes up and empty out the suitcases.

We were exhausted from our wedding day and the five-hour train trip, so we decided to take a short nap before having some lunch. After an hour of rest, we showered and got dressed and went to the lobby to get some information on where we could get a light lunch. The staff recommended a small restaurant a block and a half away. We just had a ham and cheese sandwich and a Coke because we were planning to have dinner at the hotel that evening. As we entered the hotel after lunch, we met a handsome couple from South Carolina, Elizabeth and James Johnson. They were newlyweds too and also had planned to have dinner at the hotel. Since dinner was four hours away, we decided to go back to our rooms and to meet in three hours to have a drink before dinner was served. Back in our room, Tom and I looked at the hotel's schedule. The trip planned for the next day was to go see the falls. We called the desk to make reservations for that trip.

We then got dressed to meet Elizabeth and James and went to the cocktail room. They already had the table and had waited for us to order. I told them that we had made reservations to see the falls the following day. After we ordered a drink, James got up and went to the desk to make their reservation for the trip to the falls for the following day also.

When he got back, our drinks had just arrived. I very seldom drank, but I ordered a Brandy Alexander, which was very creamy and tasty. Tom and Elizabeth had a Seven and Seven, and James had a scotch and water. We spoke about our families. James had his own clothing store business. Elizabeth was a secretary for a lawyer. They were a lovely couple.

Our dinners were great. Tom and I had a complete steak dinner. James and his wife had lobster tails. Later that evening, there was a live band, which we stayed and listen to for a while. On the next day, we met for breakfast before boarding the bus to see the falls. It was very interesting to see the falls and the other sites.

The following day, we took it easy and walked around the area. We met for an early dinner at an Italian restaurant and started off with a fine glass of red wine. The spaghetti and meatballs weren't bad for eating them out. At the end of the meal, Tom and James had demitasse with a shot of sambuca. Elizabeth and I decided to have plain vanilla ice cream with crème de mint. That was very soothing. We said our good-byes and exchanged addresses. What a lovely couple. We corresponded for many years about our children.

The following day, we left for home. My brother John met us at the Poughkeepsie train station. He parked in front of our apartment and helped us with our luggage.

We went up the narrow stairs leading to our apartment. The kitchen was so cheerful and welcoming. My brother dropped our luggage in the bedroom, and as he left, I thanked him for picking us up. We changed into comfortable clothes. Tom was thirsty for a beer, and I had a Coke. We had bought them the week of our wedding to make sure we had something cold on our arrival at home to quench our thirst. When we opened the refrigerator, we saw it was packed with food too. The pantry was as well. My mother-in-law was responsible for this good deed. She was a very kind person. It was nice having her living downstairs on the first floor. We had been home just ten minutes when she came to tell us that she had prepared dinner for us that evening.

She had made her favorite veal cutlets with roasted potatoes and fresh string beans in a pepper sauce and a delicious salad. It sure was a treat. I went to work the following Monday. Yes, our working days were ahead of us. That Sunday was Tom's turn to work at the gas station. His brother John needed a break after working alone while we were on our honeymoon.

I had to get used to the noise of the traffic on 9W. Tom was already used to it. It was quite noisy in our bedroom since it was located in the front of the apartment, facing 9W. It didn't take too long to adjust.

Our wedding day

Our First Days as Mr. and Mrs.

Joe, who drove Gaye and me to work, picked me up in front of Joe McCourt's house on King Street. It was more convenient than waiting on 9W with the morning traffic. Gaye was already in the car, having been picked up on Western Avenue. I finally got to the office. It was nice to be back with the girls. They all greeted me as soon as I walked in. They told me that it had been a beautiful wedding and that they had enjoyed it very much.

Since I got home before Tom, I would start dinner. That first night, I baked two baking potatoes, cooked fresh string beans in a delicious pepper sauce, and had steak ready for the broiler. I heard Tom come up the stairs and into the kitchen as I was opening a can of black olives. I turned and was greeted with a short kiss. Tom then went into the bathroom to take a quick shower. The potatoes were done, and I put the steaks under the broiler.

Shortly, the table was set, and so was the food. Tom said grace, and we started with our salad. After dinner, Tom went down to the gas station to give John a chance to have his dinner. Then it was John's turn to come back to work until 9:00 p.m. When Tom came upstairs after John returned from his dinner, we chatted for a while. He was working with Local 137 and operating the roller on an IBM building site in Poughkeepsie.

Tom mentioned that John had told him that someone was building a large building and needed a place to get rid of some dirt. At the time the gas station was very narrow where the gas pumps were located. John had suggested that Tom rent a dump truck and get as many loads of dirt as were available. John would take care of the business. Many loads of dirt were obtained that next day and for a few days after. The area around the pumps was widened. Cars were now able to go on both sides of the gas pumps. They worked very hard together and put in many hours. John would open at 5:30 a.m. and stay until 9:00 p.m. or later. Tom would go on his construction job at 6:00 a.m. and work every other night until 9:00 p.m. and every other Sunday. Tom also worked in between as a part-time police officer for the town.

One day at the end of June, just about a month after we were married, I felt sick to my stomach. I'd had a ham sandwich that day for lunch and wasn't sure if that was what had upset me. When Tom came home from work, he took me first to Dr. Scott's office who then referred me to the emergency room. The nurse drew blood, and after the doctor checked it, he said that I needed surgery. At eleven o'clock that evening, I had some exploratory surgery done. It was determined that my appendix was on the verge of rupturing. Until this day, ham is not one of my favorite foods. I was very lucky, as I had taken out a family plan after our marriage with Blue Cross through my company. I remember making just one payment for $4. It covered all my hospital expense and the surgeon. It sure was a large savings.

My brother Tony didn't know I had insurance and came down to ask Tom and me if we needed financial help for the hospital and surgeon. We told him that we were covered with Blue Cross. He still felt that it was his job to look out for me. He still put his family first even though I was now grown and married. We sure appreciated his concern and were fortunate not to have to rely on his offer to help us.

I stayed home for a couple of weeks and then went back to work at the office. Tom continued his work on construction and kept his schedule at the gas station. There was a diner operated by Harry Lyons and later by James Woodward next to the gas station. John and Tom thought it would be a good idea to buy the diner since it would provide more room to expand the gas station.

My sister Millie was living in North Carolina. On one of her long weekends visiting my sister Mary in Long Island, she met the man who would become her husband, Robert Sadler. He worked with Mary's husband on the docks. After a six-month courtship Bob and Millie married in Charleston, North Carolina, and lived there for a short time. But my brothers really wanted Millie to move back to the area. After Bob got to talking to my brothers, he felt he might like to work on construction as my brothers did. They soon came home for a week to visit. Bob got to meet John Arborio from Local 825 who said Bob could start working there as soon as he settled. To everyone's pleasure they moved to Marlboro. Their first apartment was in my aunt's farmhouse. They also lived in my brother Carmen's apartment on West Street and finally in their present home on White Street.

After Bob and Millie moved to Marlboro, Bob Sr. made many friends in a very short time. He belonged to the Marlboro Yacht Club. Boats and anything to do with the water were his favorite pastimes. Bob was also a very good storyteller. Bob passed away on July 7, 2010, at the age of ninety-three. He was honored and respected to the very end. Whenever you visited his home, Bob was so hospitable. He is greatly missed.

The Beginning of Our Family

IN DECEMBER OF 1947, I was expecting my first child. The first three months were miserable. The morning sickness was more than I could bear. Dr. Scott gave me some pills, and they helped to a certain degree. As I started my fourth month, I started to feel better.

I gave notice to the office that I would no longer be a part of the staff. I thanked them for the time I had been received so graciously and for making my work so enjoyable. We kept in touch by phone.

The bitter winter was gone, the spring flowers were in bloom, and everything was coming to life. Spring is my favorite season. I got busy doing spring cleaning, as I wanted to have a relaxing summer.

Tom was busy working on construction and with his brother John in the gas station. John was to get married on June 13 to Fannie Porpiglia. Tom got permission to take a week off from construction to take care of the gas station so John and Fannie would be able to take a honeymoon.

I was in my seventh month of pregnancy when I started feeling unwell again. I started to hemorrhage, and Dr. Scott had me put right away into the delivery room at St. Luke's Hospital. Tom was waiting downstairs with his mom and was very anxious. They had the incubator ready for they were sure that I would have the baby. This was my first pregnancy, and I didn't know what to expect. But I wasn't in any labor pain. However, the other mothers who were ready to give birth sure were in pain. There were all kinds of sounds, and I thought to myself, *They are putting on.* I found out later that wasn't the case. As I was lying in bed, I heard someone walking near the delivery room. The way the person walked sounded familiar. I then heard the nurse say, "I'm sorry—you're not allowed in here." Yes, it was Tom, and he told the nurse he just wanted to see me for a minute. He poked his head in the door and said, "I love you" and then had to leave. Five minutes later, the nurse brought me a small note from him. I still have the note after sixty-two years. It's saved with all my special mementos.

Dr. Scott finally realized that I wasn't going to have the baby at that time and said I had to remain in the hospital for ten days to rest and get a special injection to hold the baby. But I was very depressed in the hospital and signed myself out after three days. Dr. Scott came to my home every morning to give me that injection. I had to stay in bed without getting up for any reason. I listened very carefully to the doctor, and on August 22, I had real labor pains. I was still two weeks early. I went into labor at 7:00 a.m. and had Kathy at 5:00 p.m. It was a very difficult birth. She was born with the cord wrapped twice around her neck. You could actually see the red lines around her neck. She weighed in at six pounds and was twenty-one inches long. I was in shock when I was told it was a girl. Tom's uncle had always told me that I was carrying a boy from the shape of my stomach. I don't know why I was so sure it would be a boy. When I was told it was a girl, I told the doctor that my husband wanted a boy, and the nurse piped in and said, "Don't worry—the men determine the sex." This made me felt better.

After the first day in the hospital, I had postpartum. I was especially sad when I heard the bells ring from St. Patrick's Church. I was unable to eat, and I was getting the nurses mixed up. The following is very hard for me to write about. I told the doctor that I wanted to go home. He said the baby would have to remain in the hospital. I signed myself out. I cried all the way home from the hospital. At that time they showed the babies at a certain times of the day. Since I was unable to go to the hospital, as I was in bed with pills for my condition, Tom and his sister Anne would go twice a day to see baby Kathy. She finally came home to her beautiful crib, which was in my room. My mother-in-law helped me, Tom got up for the two o'clock feedings, and I started to get stronger and devoted my full time to my beautiful baby.

While going through postpartum, I was down to 111 pounds. Dr. Scott told me that if I didn't start to gain weight and feel stronger, I would have to go to a healthy rest home. I couldn't think of being taken away from my baby. Between the pills from Dr. Scott and forcing myself to eat good meals and milkshakes, bananas, and sweets, I started to gain some weight back. I wanted to get better for my baby and husband.

My husband was very understanding through this whole ordeal. God bless him for his patience and the love that he showed me and our daughter Kathy. Things were going in the right direction. Everything seemed so bright, and our home was full of joy. It was time to start planning for our baby's baptism. We called the rectory for this important occasion and set the date. Tom's brother John was the godfather, and my friend Gaye was the godmother. Father Hanley performed the beautiful ceremony. We then gathered at my house for dinner. Kathy slept while we had dinner. She woke up after we had the delicious cake. I went in the room and found her in her crib; she was wide awake, looking all around the room. She still had her baptism dress on, and I quickly changed her diaper and took off her dress and put a white kimono on her while Tom was heating the bottle. I gave her the bottle, and she was really hungry. She took a couple of good burps. After two hours she went back to sleep. Tom and I cleaned the dinner dishes and finally called it an early night. We thanked the Lord for such a beautiful day.

The time seemed to go by fast. I was busy with my home and tending to Kathy. Tom was busy with his work. Every other Sunday, Tom had a day off. We would take Kathy to Downing Park in Newburgh to feed the ducks. Of course we would always take our camera with us. After spending some time in the park, we would take her for lunch and then go home to put her down for a nap.

When Kathy was three years old, we enrolled her in Eckie's Nursery School on Plattekill Road in Marlboro. She enjoyed it very much. After dinner she was allowed to watch *Howdy Doody*. I would then bathe her, put her pajamas on, read her a story, and put her to bed.

On Tom's night off we would discuss what had taken place during the day or be invited downstairs to Tom's parents' home for some dessert. We would keep our bedroom door open so we could hear Kathy if she woke up, although once she fell asleep, she always slept through the whole night. After our dessert we would come up and check on Kathy and get ready for a restful night.

Our Second Daughter

N 1952 I GAVE BIRTH to my second beautiful daughter, Donna Maria. I must say it was a much more pleasant pregnancy. I had very little morning sickness. My prayers were answered that I would be able to remain in the hospital with the baby. Donna had a beautiful smile from the early months. I remember when Tom came to pick me up at the hospital, he brought Kathy with him. I was sitting in the wheelchair holding the new baby. Kathy seemed confused as she stared at her new sister. I bent over to kiss her so that she did not feel left out.

Tom was happy that the baby and I were at home. Kathy was mom's helper. This made her feel very important. Of course in those days there were no diaper services or prepackaged diapers as there are today. We bought cloth diapers and washed and sterilized them. The milk bottles also had to be sterilized before being filled with the formula. I had a break whenever my sister-in-law Fannie would take Kathy along with her son, Anthony, for a walk.

Preparations were made for Donna Maria's baptism. Aunt Fannie Amodeo was the godmother, and cousin Tony (Zack) Amodeo was the godfather. Father Hanley also did the ceremony, and we had a small reception at our home.

As Donna got older, Fannie and I and our husbands managed to go out for late Saturday dinners. It was usually the Marlo Inn, Ship Lantern Inn, or the Coppola Brothers, who had their restaurant on Main Street in Poughkeepsie. Coppola's was the best Italian restaurant in the area. It was operated by three Coppola boys who married the three Mazzella girls.

We would always start with their hot antipasto and an entrée of veal, chicken, or eggplant with a good-sized order of spaghetti with the best sauce. The garlic bread and red wine were a must. The portions were so large that we always had a take-home container. This one Saturday evening, my sister-in-law Anne babysat for Kathy and Donna. For some reason, Donna cried, and Anne was unable to stop her. They called my sister Millie, and finally Donna stopped crying. Her aunt Millie became her confirmation godmother years later.

Again on Tom's Sunday off we would take both girls to Downing Park to feed the ducks, take pictures, and have a light lunch. It was difficult raising the children in our apartment because there was no play yard. We had to be very careful when we were outside because of 9W and cars coming and going out of the gas station. We usually sat on Tom's parents' porch, with a gate in front of the entrance to the porch to make sure the kids wouldn't run out and get hit by a car.

Whenever my sister Mary visited from Long Island, she would always bring gifts for my girls. I remember this beautiful mint dress she brought for Donna. I dressed her up and went to sit on the porch, and her uncle John just couldn't resist her. She always had this beautiful smile, and he was tempted to pick her up and hug and kiss her but stopped short when he realized his hands were full of grease as he was in the middle of working on a car.

Things were going very smoothly with the children, and our extended families were all doing well. The families were growing larger.

Our Family Is Complete

IN 1955 WE HAD ANOTHER surprise; we would be adding another child to our family. When I went for my 8ᵗʰ month checkup, the doctor told me the baby had a fast heartbeat. Kathy and Donna had both had fast heartbeats too. I was really hoping for a boy this time, not for me, but for my husband.

Kathy at the time was in second grade, and Donna was at nursery school. I kept busy helping Kathy with her Baltimore catechism and learning her prayers as she prepared to make her first Holy Communion. Her cousin, Anthony Amodeo, also made his first Holy Communion, and a party was combined for them.

When the summer was over, and we could feel the fall in the air, I got all my fall cleaning done, knowing November would be here soon, and a new member would be added to our family. We got the crib ready for that special day, and I had the baby bottles and nipples sterilized. I always tried to be well organized. November 11, 1955, arrived, and I started to get labor pains. Tom took me to the hospital. Dr. Scott told me it wouldn't be long. The nurse relayed the message to Tom, who was in the waiting room awaiting the birth of the baby.

I told Dr. Scott not to tell me if it was a girl. I knew the time was here for the baby to enter the world as the nurse put a mask on me that contained ether to dull the pain. Well, at last the baby arrived, and Dr. Scott didn't say a word. I waited a couple of minutes and asked him, "Is it another girl?"

He responded, "She is beautiful." I didn't have any kind words for him. I must say she was a beautiful baby—eight pounds, twelve ounces. Today, Cindy is the daughter that every parent would want. In fact the Lord blessed me with three lovely daughters. They are always there for my husband and me. He was always proud of his girls.

Tom with our daughters: Kathy (standing), Cindy (left), and Donna (right)

Our Home

THE FAMILY WAS GETTING TOO large for the apartment, and we decided that we would have to look for some property. We were definitely in need of a bigger home and a backyard where the children would have a safe place to play. Since John and Fannie's family was also growing, they were interested in buying property too. At the time they had two boys, Anthony and Johnnie-Boy.

After looking around, we found property owned by Rocco Mautone on the corner of Orange and Bloom Streets. We did like the location, as it was just out of town but close enough to walk to church, the post office, and the grocery stores. Neither Fannie nor I drove at that time. After much consideration we decided to buy the property. Our next step was to get a house plan and a builder. At the time Paul Giglia was building quite a few new homes. I had happened to graduate high school with him, and I didn't realize he was now a builder for residential homes. We got in touch with him, and he showed us homes that he had built in Newburgh and New Windsor. In fact, he had built my brother Tony's house. We were impressed by his work. He used the best materials.

Fannie and I both liked the same plan that Paul showed us for a brick ranch. The contract called for cast iron heat, plaster walls, excellent wood for our hardwood floors, custom-made kitchen cabinets, and brick to finish off the outside of the house. The homes were built in 1956, and the workmanship was excellent. At the time Anthony and Albert Pagano were doing the brickwork for Paul, and their work was also excellent. I still live in this home.

Johnnie-Boy took over his father's house when he got married to Joyce Logue. Fannie and I enjoyed the many years she lived next door. We would have our coffee together every morning and at the same time would write out our grocery list. We would call the order into Marlboro Beef grocery store, and the groceries would be delivered. Joe Pesavento was the proprietor, and he was a fine gentleman. Joe and I shared the same birthday, and we sometimes would go to dinner with him and his wife at the Ship Lantern Inn or Coppola's.

Not only did Fannie and I have our morning coffee and write out our grocery lists together, but we always shared the same car and even the same dog too. It worked out very well. Soon John and Fannie had another addition to the family, a beautiful girl named Deborah. Fannie was not well after her birth, so I would give Deborah the two o'clock feeding. The phone would ring once, and I would go over to change her diaper and feed her. After a couple of burps, she was ready to go back to sleep.

As a youngster Johnnie-Boy sure kept our daughter Cindy and our neighbor April Presler in line. He liked to play war with his small group of plastic soldiers, and he would line them all up outside. Once, the girls knocked them over. They never did it again.

One day my brother Tony's wife Rose had some minor surgery. Tony was working for Local 825. He asked me to take care of his two daughters, Michele and Gerri. I was very happy to do so. They were practically the same age as Donna and Cindy, and they had all played very well until this one day.

Our neighbor, Mr. Bill Riley, had two small buildings behind my house. He used one as a chicken coop and the other for his rabbit. Mr. Riley had left some paint and brushes near the chicken coop. When I checked on the girls from my back window, Gerri and Cindy were painting the coop. It was all so streaky, and they had covered most of the coop. I was so angry that I started to cry. I didn't know what to do. When Mr. Riley came home that afternoon, I went to see him and explained the situation. He knew how upset I was and told me not to be worried, as he was going to tear them down.

I sat down with the girls, who were five years old at that time, and told them how wrong it was to do what they had done. They were not allowed to look at TV that evening and had to go to bed early. I had to use gas to remove the white paint from their hands and faces. I had to discard their clothes.

Cindy wasn't the last addition to our family. In 1966 I received a phone call from my sister Mary from Long Island telling me that her youngest daughter, Anne Marie, was not well. Mary was a widow who had been left with eight children when her husband passed from lung cancer at forty-eight years old.

Tom and I talked it over and decided we both would be happy to have Anne Marie come live with us. She started the fourth grade here and was a good student and very obedient. She got along very well with her cousins.

After six weeks, she returned to her doctor in Long Island for a checkup. The first thing the doctor asked was, "Who is taking care of this girl?" She had gained two pounds and had a healthy color. She came back after the doctor's visit and stayed with us a total of six years, until her sophomore year of high school, when her mother took ill and needed her home. Her mother did miss her very much. Her teacher, Mr. Mirra, was disappointed she was leaving.

After moving back, she attended John Adam's High School in Jamaica, where she graduated. She's doing well, working for an insurance company. She married and divorced. She helps her sister take care of my sister Mary, her mom, who is now ninety-three years old. Anne Marie showed her love and appreciation to us. She was here to support the family after Tom was in a car accident, and she was at his bedside as he went home to the Lord.

Vacationing with the Amodeos

In 1963 Fannie and I got our driver's licenses. This was necessary, as our husbands worked many hours, and we had to take over. From then on, in July of every year, Fannie and I would drive the children to the Jersey Shore. Our husbands were too busy with the gas station and with construction. That worked very well.

February was a good time for Tom and John to have some R&R. Many years, we went to Jamaica. Albert Pagano was in charge of the gas station while we were gone. One year we went to Italy. Gaye and Howard Van Etten (Gaye's second husband) came along on this trip. Howard had been stationed in Italy during the war. We rented a large van, and Howard was the driver. On this particular trip Tom and John wanted to go to Monteforte, where they were born. They showed us the house where they had lived, the places they had played with their friends, and a very old cemetery. They were so excited to show us the town.

Many of the people they knew no longer lived there; they had moved to the cities. I knew that my father's sister was living there, so as we drove through the town, I stopped to ask someone where Lucia Pasquale lived. They gave us directions to her home, which was at the end of town. Howard drove very slowly, and I spotted a woman wearing a kerchief around her head. She had on a long black cotton dress with a short apron and a black sweater over it. She was short and dark-skinned. She was coming out of the house as we approached. We got out of the van, and I walked toward her. I asked if she was Lucia Pasquale, and she answered, "Si, si." I told her that I was the daughter of Michael Pasquale from America. She got so happy and immediately began hugging and kissing me. Once my father left Italy, he hadn't made a trip back. We were all invited inside. It was a damp day, and a cup of coffee with some kind of liquor poured into it warmed us up a bit. She wanted me to stay overnight, but I told her Howard had made some other plans. I took a picture with her, and I showed it to my sisters and brothers. I know if my father hadn't died so young, he would have made the trip back to visit his birthplace. We said our good-byes to Lucia and left.

The next day, Howard drove us to Germany. Tom and John showed us the different places they were stationed during the war. I remember Tom pointing out one of the cities as we passed the sign pointing to Frankfurt. One day before this portion of our trip was to end, Howard took us through the Alps. We hit a terrible blizzard. It was so dangerous that we couldn't see the side of the road, but we knew there was a big drop. We knew if we skidded, that would be the end. We girls grasped our rosaries and started to pray. Howard, being a Methodist, was amused. However, he was very careful, and thank God, we were finally safe.

We still had five days left before we had to head home. Fannie said she had some relations in Sicily, and Howard was happy to make the plans. We took a train and stayed in Palermo. I must say that Sicily was beautiful.

In the following years we went to Spain, Greece, Austria, Mexico, and other different places. Howard could really read a map. During the war, Howard was in the Air Force, and for his service to our country, he received the Medal of Honor. When he passed away, there was a small table near his casket where the medal was placed. His sister-in-law brought it from Highland Mills. May he rest in peace.

Faith Sustains Me Again

ALL THE CHILDREN WERE DOING well in school and certainly getting older. One day Tom was working on construction on the IBM building. I was in the kitchen getting ready to prepare dinner for that evening when I noticed a car coming up the drive. I looked out the window and saw Tom sitting in the passenger seat. I rushed out to the car to see what the problem was. The construction worker who brought Tom home said he was having severe pains in his stomach. He helped Tom into the house, and I immediately called the doctor, who told me to bring him to the ER by ambulance. On the way to the hospital, Tom suffered internal bleeding. I remember the ambulance driver putting on the sirens and really speeding en route to St. Luke's.

Once we got to the hospital, things were very critical. Doctors were coming in and out of his room, and nurses were bringing in bags of blood to give him transfusions. I sat there with Tom in the hospital bed, knowing that things were bad. He was losing the blood as it was being administered. I was told to get the children and family to the hospital. The girls were at the school watching a basketball game. A priest was called in to give him the last rites of the Catholic Church.

It was seven o'clock that evening when Dr. Wahl said they had no choice but to operate. We were to wait until twelve o'clock that evening, hoping that the bleeding would subside. Doctors usually would not operate if the bleeding hadn't stopped. Tom seemed to be resting peacefully, and I left the room. I went into the adjoining room because I didn't want him to know that I was staying overnight. I took out my rosary and spoke to our Lord, asking for Tom to get better. I rested for a while, and then a figure dressed in white entered the room to tell me that the bleeding had subsided. It was Marion Casey from Marlboro, who was a nurse at St. Luke's. They continued the blood transfusions until he got strong enough for them to operate. Tom's brother John had asked the surgeon, Dr. Wahl, if he could get a second opinion from a New York City surgeon. The doctor replied, "It's too late." Dr. Wahl said that they were doing all they could at this time. John and my family were there to help me and my siblings.

I went into the room as Tom lay among the white sheets. He was so pale from all the blood he had lost that his complexion blended in with the sheets. I said I was going home to see the girls before they left for school. My sister Millie and sister-in-law Fannie had been taking care of them while I stayed at the hospital.

My brother-in-law, Bob Sadler, picked me up. I remember the joy I felt that there was some improvement, although the doctor had told me Tom wasn't out of the woods yet.

On the ride home, the sky was a beautiful blue, and I just had a feeling that things were going to be fine. But then I started to fear the worst. What would I do without Tom and the children without a father? As we were approaching St. Mary's, I asked Bob if he would stop so I could go in and light a candle. He was happy to do that favor.

As I entered the church, I got a peaceful feeling that told me the Lord would answer my prayer and Tom would be fine. Our Lady looking down from the side altar gave me that beautiful smile. As I left the church, it was quite dark inside, and the red candle holders gave a beautiful red glow. The blue candle holders gave off a calming blue glow.

I left full of the Holy Spirit. I got home, and the girls were very sad. I told them to keep praying and that their dad was doing slightly better. I took a rest and then went back to the hospital. I met with Dr. Wahl, and he told me they would operate the following day. I must say I was very nervous. I went the following morning before the surgery. The nurses got Tom ready, and minutes later, a male nurse came with a stretcher, and Tom was gently placed on it. I bent over and gave him a short kiss. His green eyes always said it all. "Don't worry," they said this time, but of course I did.

During three hours of surgery, the cause of the bleeding was found to be a small hole in the artery leading to the heart. In order for this to heal he had to be on a special diet, medication and rest for a month. After the month, Tom had another x-ray taken, and things looked great. I had my husband back. Thank God.

Around this time, I started to teach religious instructions. I had the children who were preparing to make their First Holy Communion. During this time Father Hanley was our parish priest. For my first class, I helped the teacher. The class had fifteen to twenty children in it. It wasn't until later, after my girls were all in school, that I worked along with Msgr. Simmons and Father Dugan. The classes were getting very large. Later, Fannie Amodeo and I would work together. It was very rewarding to teach these innocent children. Preparing them for Holy Communion was my favorite. Many of these children, who are now parents, remember me as their religious teacher. They have families of their own now. I also belonged to the Catholic Daughters in my earlier years.

In my later years, the Legion of Mary was started in our church. There were seven members, and we met every Tuesday. We would attend mass and hold a short prayer session followed by a short meeting. We also went, two or three of us in a group, to visit the sick in the hospital or at home. After many years, some members passed away or became sick. Anna Swain and I are the only two survivors at this time. One of the members was Concetta Mazzella. Whenever she visited the Italian-speaking patients, she would pray with them in Italian and give them words of encouragement. She always ended a visit by singing "Ave Maria" in Italian, and the patients were happy with her visits. Other members were Kathy Wassi, Molly Guiccardo, Kathy Scott, and Mary Lupi—beautiful ladies!

Our girls were getting older, and there were always friends at our home for sleepovers. Tom was surrounded by all these girls. I must say they favored Tom, as he would always joke with them. I had certain rules that had to be followed. But they always had a good time. My nephew Anthony Amodeo was a handsome boy and always had a group of girls from his class visiting, including Julie VanVliet, Linda Canosa, Lori Lee Bull, and Ruth Anne McQuiston. They always hung out together. He married one of the girls, Julie VanVliet, after he graduated from Marquette University. Early on, I had a feeling that she would someday be his wife. Julie graduated from Elizabeth Seton College and Mount Saint Mary College. After teaching and serving as an administrator, she became superintendent of schools. Anthony also did very well. After teaching he became vice president of BOCES in Ulster County. They have a beautiful daughter, Alicia, and a son-in-law, Jay.

KATHY AND DONNA GET MARRIED

KATHY

WHEN KATHY WAS SIXTEEN, SHE was given a beautiful party at St. Mary's Hall. About 100 people attended. The hall was decorated in pink and white streamers, and tables covered in white had a vase with pink flowers in the center, and the tables covered in pink contained a vase with white flowers. Kathy wore a pink dress with a wrist corsage made of pink and white rose buds. The food was catered by Sal's from Newburgh, and soft drinks were served. Dancing was enjoyed by all.

Kathy graduated from high school a year before her cousin Anthony, with whom she was very close. While in high school she belonged to the drama club and was a cheerleader. She graduated from Ulster County Community College and took courses at Mount Saint Mary College in Newburgh. She became a secretary at IBM and bought a Pontiac to drive back and forth to work. She started dating Gordon Ronk, who also attended Ulster Community College and was taking up mechanics. He eventually taught at a regional/career/technical center.. They courted for about a year and got engaged. A beautiful diamond was bought at the Diamond Center in New York. It was just about a perfect diamond.

It wasn't long before a wedding date was announced for Satuday, October 25, 1969. It sure was a busy time around the Tom Amodeo household. Plans were made for a reception at the Meadowbrook Lodge in New Windsor. The church ceremony at St. Mary's was held scheduled at four o'clock. Since it was a candlelight wedding, we couldn't have it earlier. On the sills in front of the beautiful stained glass windows were candles surrounded by fall flowers. Every third pew had a standing white candle with greens and a white bow in the center of the holder. At each side of the altar was a large candle holder with greens and bows streaming down. She had a large wedding party made up of mostly female cousins and two friends. They all wore burgundy fine velvet gowns with a tapestry band at the waist and bottom of the gowns. On their heads they wore the tapestry material made into a stand-up brim with short netting. This carried out the matching band on the gown. The tapestry was off-white with small green and burgundy flowers. Each bridesmaid carried fall flowers with a burgundy candle in a clear glass holder at the center, which gave off a beautiful glow. Many candles were needed to give that glow, as all the overhead lights were out for this candlelight wedding.

I wore a beautiful light purple velvet gown with a mink stole that my husband had purchased for me the year before. The gown was tight at the waist with a full skirt, short sleeves, and a square neckline. I wore silver shoes and matching bag, and on my wrist was a beautiful white orchid with a silver bow. My husband was easy to take care of. He wore a miniature carnation in the lapel of the tux for which he'd been fitted. It was just as easy for the best man and ushers; they all ordered their tuxedos and wore a miniature carnation on their lapels as well. Paul Ligouri was Gordon's best friend, so he was the best man.

Kathy wore a "Camelot" gown made by Lucretia's Bridal Shop on Broadway in Newburgh. Lucretia was an outstanding designer. Kathy was 5'7" tall and wore her gown beautifully. The high collar was made of a very fine satin, as was the rest of the gown except for the bodice part, which was made of imported Italian lace. The gown also had long sleeves, a tight waist, and a semiflare. She had a long fine veil with a long train. Her headpiece matched the fine Italian lace. Her hair came to the top of her shoulders. She carried a beautiful bouquet of white roses. Donna, her sister, was maid of honor and looked awesome as she walked gracefully down the aisle.

The photographer was Bill Galati. As the limos waited patiently many pictures were taken. When we were ready to leave the house and head to the church, Tom sat in front with the limo driver, and Kathy, Donna, and I sat in the back. The groom and ushers were already in church. The groom's mother, Babe Ronk, was already waiting in the lobby of the church.

At the church, Donna helped Kathy out of the car and with her long veil. I started to walk up the church steps. I was already ten minutes late. At that point Mrs. Ronk was escorted down the aisle by one of the ushers. A couple of minutes later, my nephew, Anthony Amodeo, walked me down the aisle to my seat in the front row. The bridesmaids were all in the back of the church. The ushers took their places in church along with the best man and groom.

Msgsr. Simmons was in front of the altar as the organ music began. We all stood up and watched as the beautiful attendants came down the aisle with their lighted candles. With their glow and the glow from the window candles, it was a beautiful picture. The attendants placed their lighted candles surrounded by fall flowers on the altar to give light to Msgr. for his readings.

Finally, Kathy and her handsome dad walked down the aisle. They walked slowly, and I must add that Kathy looked regal. When they got to the front of the altar, her dad gently drew the veil over her face and fixed it gently and neatly. Her husband-to-be was there beside her. Gordon looked very handsome. The ceremony started, and Msgr. John Simmons performed a beautiful ceremony in which he spoke about the importance of a marriage. They both took their wedding vows very seriously. When the ceremony was over, they smiled at their guests in a packed church as they walked down the aisle to the top of the stairs in front of the church.

It was time to get into the limos for the ride to the reception at Meadowbrook Lodge in New Windsor. It took much time for the full wedding party to get there because there were twenty of them. The bride and groom and their attendants had their own private room for the cocktail hour. The rest of the guests were in the side-room annex to the large reception room for the cocktail hour. Once the hour was over, the guests entered the main room, finding their tables as they entered. When all the guests were settled, the members of the bridal party lined up to enter the main room as their names were called. The band played a short tune as each couple entered and stood in line in the middle of the dance floor. Once all their names had been called, Tom and I, maid of honor Donna, best man Paul Liguori, and then the important ones of the evening, Mr. and Mrs. Gordon Ronk, were announced. The bridal couple danced to "Till," which was their song. A toast was given, and dinner was served: soup, salad, and a choice of filet mignon, chicken, or fish with roasted potatoes and a choice of string beans or asparagus for the vegetable. Wine, soda, and beer were served with dinner. Dinner music played as everyone enjoyed their meal, and dancing continued for most of the evening.

The wedding cake, from Café Aurora in Poughkeepsie, was topped with whipped cream and cannoli filling. A miniature bride and groom stood on top. There was still half an hour left before eleven o'clock when the bride and groom thanked everyone for coming. The dancing continued, and the guests were having such a good time that my husband extended the band for a half-hour longer. In the meantime the bride and groom had left for their honeymoon at Paradise Island in the Bahamas.

It sure was a long day and night for us. We were happy that all went well. Their home was ready for them when they came home from their trip. It was a beautiful five-room house on the end of Orange Street, just down the street from my home. It was purchased from Sheldon Edmond and his wife, an elderly couple who had no children and were going to live with their niece. The house had been built by Mr. Arthur Barley and Sons and had been kept so well that the newlyweds could just move in. The landscaping was beautifully maintained. The backyard had two beautiful white oak trees plus beautiful flowers. They sure had a good start in married life. Kathy continued to work at IBM, and at the time Gordon worked at Floyd's TNT.

After the wedding, things were pretty much the same at home. Donna and Cindy were in high school. Tom and I were taking our winter vacation with John, Fannie, Gaye, and Howard. Our social life consisted of going out for dinner on Saturday nights or attending weddings or other affairs. After four years, Kathy was pregnant, and we were very happy for the good news. Unfortunately, she had a miscarriage at the beginning of the pregnancy. We were all very sad, and Kathy was devastated.

DONNA

Donna had graduated from high school and Dutchess Community College and was dating her high school sweetheart, Vincent Porcelli.

He was attending Upstate Center Syracuse Medical School. On the weekends, he worked at the college and studied. The first time I met Vinnie was at St. Mary's religion class, which is where I met my son-in-law Gordon Ronk as well, in the same class.

I was teaching that class when Vinnie and his twin brother Frank started throwing spitballs in class. I stopped the class and said to them, "Just look at Gordon Ronk and how he is paying attention and not causing any disturbance in this class." They apologized; however, I felt a phone call to their dad would prevent any more of this foolishness. That evening I called Mr. Ed Porcelli and told him of the incident. I told him if he just spoke to them and didn't punish them severely, that would take care of the problem.

However, their dad didn't completely take my advice; they were both punished severely. That took care of the problem, and they were well behaved thereafter. Today Vinnie is Deacon Porcelli at St. Mary's and Our Lady of Mercy.

Soon Donna and Vinnie were engaged, and their wedding was to take place on May 13, 1971. They planned on renting an apartment in Syracuse until Vinnie completed his studies and graduated.

I was back in the picture of planning another wedding. It wasn't difficult, as I had learned a lot from Kathy's wedding. We first made the reservations for the church, the reception, the photographer, the limos, and the rehearsal dinner. St. Mary's, of course, would be the church. The Meadowbrook Lodge was once again chosen for the reception as it was the most popular place at the time. Galati's, which was known to take many pictures of the bride, was chosen for the albums.

One Saturday, Donna, her aunt Millie, and I went to Lucretia's on Broadway in Newburgh. Donna wanted a simpler gown than her sister Kathy had. She chose a fine satin material. The dress featured short sleeves, and the bodice to the fitted waist was a fine lace. A semistraight skirt was formed from fine satin from the waist down. It looked like the gown was glued to her body. She looked stunning. Her long hair passed the square collar to her shoulders. A beautiful dozen white roses with babies breath and green fern went beautifully with her headpiece, which was a beaded band attached to her fingertip veil. The attendants' gowns were purchased in the same bridal store. Kathy was her matron of honor, and a few of her cousins and friends were the attendants. They wore pale blue gowns with a pink band around the waist.

When the big day arrived, I had a full house as the attendants dressed and had their hair and makeup done at our home. The photographer waited patiently to take pictures of the bride and her attendants. Meanwhile, I was getting dressed in my beautiful blue silk dress. I picked blue for Our Lady's color since May was the month of the Holy Rosary. Tom was already dressed in his tux and looked as handsome as ever.

Since the attendants were not quite ready, Mr. Galati took some shots of Tom and me with the bride. When the attendants were all ready, many pictures were taken of the group as they posed with the bride.

It was a beautiful day. The sky was the most beautiful shade of blue. As we drove down Boom Street, I couldn't help but think of the date; it was the First Apparition of Our Lady at Fatima. As we pulled in front of our beautiful St. Mary's Church, I noticed that the ushers' limo was already parked, and the ushers, the best man (Eddie Porcelli), and the groom were already in the church.

The limo driver got out and opened the back door. I climbed out, followed by Kathy and the bride. I walked up the front steps of the church and waited at the entrance. My nephew Anthony Amodeo escorted me to my seat.

As I walked down the aisle, I couldn't help admiring how beautiful the altar looked. On either side were large baskets of white flowers with beautiful greens and a blue bow to honor Our Lady of Fatima. Every third pew had carnations hanging with the beautiful greens and white streamers. Mrs. Downer, the organist, started the music, and the guests, who practically filled the church, all stood.

The attendants started to walk down the aisle at a slow pace. The groom and best man stood tall in front of the altar, and the ushers, three on each side, stood in front of the first pew. Kathy, the matron of honor, came down the aisle very slowly and looked very regal.

After a good long space, Tom proudly walked down the aisle with his middle daughter. He was filled with much pride and love. She was very solemn and looked like a princess. At the altar, Tom picked up her veil and neatly took it from her face. He gave her a loving kiss before presenting her to Vinnie, her husband-to-be, who wore a ruffled shirt under his tux and a large bow tie. When Tom came to sit next to me at the first pew, he was emotional with teary eyes. They were tears of joy.

132

Msgr. Simmons performed a beautiful ceremony. When Vinnie and Donna walked down the aisle as man and wife, it was a joyous scene.

We got to the Meadow Brook Lodge after a very beautiful church wedding. The cocktail hour was about to start just as we arrived. Tom and I sat at a little round table and ordered a cocktail. A great selection of hors d'oeuvres was also served. The bridal party had its own private room. Frances and Ed Porcelli, the groom's parents, joined us. They were lovely people. She looked stunning in her beautiful green gown. We spent a lot of time with them because they were such a beautiful family.

The hour was finally over, and it was time for the guests to take their seats at their tables. The maître d' announced that the bridal party was ready to enter. The attendants and ushers were called in two by two while the band played a short tune. Frances and Ed and Tom and I were called next. Finally came the big announcement: Mr. and Mrs. Vincent Porcelli. They danced to their song, "More." Finally we all joined in the dance.

The bridal party went to their seats with Donna and Vinnie seated in the center. The best man gave a beautiful toast. We then began dinner with a mixed green salad. You could not hear a sound as everyone ate their dinner, which consisted of filet mignon, chicken, or fish; golden roasted potatoes were served with the beef and chicken, and rice was served with the fish. Music complemented the dinner and provided a soothing background. It wasn't long before the guests started to dance. There were rolling carts of wine and other drinks that were continuously served to the guests.

When the beautiful white cake with cannoli filling was ready to be served, the bride and groom stood next to the cake and each had a morsel. They were very neat about it. The guests were served the wedding cake with a dip of vanilla ice cream and fresh strawberries. Regular and decaf coffee were served along with the after-dinner drinks.

When there was a break in the music, Donna and Vinnie got up to thank their guests for making their special day more special. They went to Hawaii for their wedding trip. They then returned to Syracuse, where Vinnie graduated the following year. Donna continued to take extra college credits. They then moved to Monticello, where Vinnie had his first job as director of the lab at the Community General Hospital.

OUR LADY, THE BLESSED MOTHER

IT WAS OCTOBER 1971 WHEN I awoke one morning after Our Lady had come to me during the night or very early morning to tell me that I was to have a statue of her. I was somehow directed to place it by St. Mary's Church.

The morning of this beautiful dream or whatever had taken place with Our Lady, I went to see Msgr. John D. Simmons. I asked him if my husband and I could place a beautiful marble statue of Our Lady on the church property, and he answered, "Anne, you can put it anywhere you want except in the middle of the aisle." I immediately called a place in Saugerties, and the gentleman came up with his portfolio and showed us the beautiful displays of Our Lady made of Carrara marble from Italy. We ordered the statue, and in June 1972, it was placed on the right side of our beautiful St. Mary's Church. I had a light installed that would keep it lit at night. I tended to it with beautiful flowers, especially in May, October, and Christmas and all the seasons, until 2006. At this time, my husband needed attention, and I wasn't giving it fully, so I prayed about it. Then one day, my niece Debbie Adamschick asked if she could place some flowers by Our Lady. She took over and has been in charge of the statue ever since, and what a beautiful job she does. Our Lady answered my prayers.

Debbie takes such good care of the soil that the plants look artificial. In the hot summer she carries gallons of water to make sure the flowers stay healthy. I call her Mary's Angel. My mind is at ease knowing that Our Lady is taken excellent care of. Thanks, Debbie, and God bless.

The statue of Our Lady at St. Mary's Church

OUR TWENTY-FIFTH

IN 1972 TOM AND I celebrated our twenty-fifth wedding anniversary. The children gave us a beautiful surprise party at the Bell's Catering Hall in New Windsor. It was planned that we would be attending a surprise birthday party for my sister-in-law Anne DiRienzo. She was a lovely person, and we were looking forward to attending her party.

My sister-in-law Fannie insisted that we get gowns for this occasion because it was to be formal, and the gowns would be more appropriate. We both went and got gowns at Women's Wear on Broadway. I later realized that she wanted me to be dressed in something beautiful because the surprise was for me. John Repke was the photographer, and he was going to put an album together for us. My sisters Mary and Margaret attended from Long Island with their husbands. Msgr. Simmons was there to renew our vows along with Tom's best man, John, and my maid of honor, Gaye. The band played beautiful songs, including "Let Me Call You Sweetheart," which was the song we danced to at our wedding. My husband presented me with a beautiful two-carat ring combined with an interlocking wedding band set in platinum.

To make the room warm and cozy, my daughters had the round tables set with blue tablecloths with matching napkins. The centerpieces contained blue and white flowers and a silver ribbon printed with the words "Happy 25th."

The food was excellent, and having my brothers and sisters there to help me celebrate made me very happy. My sister Millie and sister-in-law Fannie had sure kept the big surprise a secret, which made it a very happy evening. Everyone had a good time.

I thanked my daughters and their husbands for such a great party. Thank God for my three beautiful daughters and their husbands.

In January of that year, we took our vacation to Switzerland. It was Gaye, Fannie, and I with our spouses. On this vacation, Joe Torraca and his wife, Sam, joined us. Our first stop was Zurich. It was a scene right off a postcard. It was snowing, and some of the Christmas decorations were still up, and the glow from the colorful lights covered the streets and sidewalks like a fantasy land.

We decided to have a late dinner so we could walk around this fantasy land, even though we were getting full of snow. We finally spotted a beautiful restaurant that had a live band performing. We decided that we would have dinner there. We were seated at a table near a large stone fireplace that had an orange burning from the inside. It was sure inviting after walking in the snow. We started our dinner with a delicious bowl of hot chicken soup. It was the best that I'd ever had. For my main course I chose a steak, prepared medium-well; potato and vegetable; and hot, buttered French bread. The best part of the dinner was the excellent red wine that was served.

The band was in full swing. The hostess came to our table and asked where we were from. We told her we were from the United States, and she must have conveyed this to the band because they started to play "Three Cheers for the USA." It was great, and we were so happy to be Americans. Of course the wine helped us to celebrate. We found out when the check came that it was $300 just for the wine. They bought the best. It was a beautiful evening, and we were tired and needed a good night's rest.

The next day, we decided that we would do some sightseeing. We made our plans to take a horse and buggy ride through the scenic woods and frozen lake and stop at a well-known restaurant. It was about five o'clock when we left. It was very cold because the sun was no longer out. We got into the buggy and covered ourselves with the blankets they supplied. As we traveled through the woods, with a full moon visible through the trees, the scene looked like a picture. The homes at the end of the frozen lake had an orange color in their windows, and you could see the smoke billowing out of the chimneys. Our wool hats felt so good covering our ears. We found ourselves within yards of that popular restaurant and were so happy to see the lights, as we were bitter cold despite having plenty of warm clothes and blankets on us.

We entered the restaurant and saw a beautiful fire crackling in the fireplace. Again we were seated by the fireplace and immediately ordered a hot toddy. That really hit the spot. We never enjoyed heat as much as that evening. We ordered a special stew that was a house favorite. It consisted of veal, potatoes, and peas in a creamy sauce. Anything that was hot and hardy was perfect for this cold evening. We dreaded the ride back to our rooms, as it was below zero.

Our First Grandchild

AFTER FOUR YEARS OF MARRIAGE, our daughter Kathy gave birth to a beautiful girl, Maria Michele. She was twenty-one inches long and six pounds five ounces. We were so delighted and thankful for this beautiful gift from our Lord. Gordon, Kathy's husband, and I sat in the waiting room and waited for the good news. When it finally came, we immediately went to the nursery and waited by the glass window. She was easy to pick out, as she had blue eyes and blonde hair. She was all Ronk. Kathy was excited with her beautiful daughter. I telephoned my husband to tell him the great news, and he passed it on to Cindy, who was attending college. I then placed a call to Donna in Syracuse. That weekend, Donna and Vinnie made the trip home to visit the new addition to our family. The baby's room was beautifully decorated for a small princess. She really was a princess to our family. I was so happy that they lived at the end of Orange Street. I would go up every day to bathe her, help make her formula, change her diapers, and help with whatever was necessary. I also had a crib in my house so I was able to babysit. I was so proud of my first grandchild.

Maria spoke at a very young age, and one morning when she came to visit, she called me "MeMa." Poppy (Tom) and I were very happy to babysit for her. Whenever her mom would come to pick her up from our house, she would run and hide, and we really enjoyed that. Her aunt Donna and aunt Cindy enjoyed her immensely too. They gave her so much love.

Soon, Maria was ready for nursery school. She also took dancing lessons and enjoyed it very much. Her favorite holiday was Christmas.

I remember that when we took down our Christmas tree after New Year's, Maria cried so much that it was difficult to console her.

Vinnie and Donna soon became parents as well. When we received the call that Donna was in labor, Tom and I went to Monticello. Our second grandchild had arrived. He was named Thomas Amodeo Porcelli. We were overjoyed. He was such a handsome little lad. He had colic for many weeks, which was very difficult for him and his parents.

Tom loved our visits with Maria and baby Tom. His namesake would cry every time we had to leave. Young Tom went to nursery school and enjoyed it very much. Vinnie and Donna then decided to move to Marlboro, and young Tom graduated from Marlboro High School, where he played football and was a very good player. He is employed at the Marlboro High School and is very popular with the students.

Our first grandchild, Maria Ronk

THE FINAL WEDDING

CINDY HAD GRADUATED FROM DUTCHESS Community College and was dating her middle school sweetheart David Schaffer. Yes, plans again were being made. This time it was for our third daughter and our last wedding. She and David were busy picking out their bridal party. We and the Schaffers were also busy making preparations. We went through the list of things that had to be planned. The church date, invitations, music, photographer, and flowers and a place for the reception had to be decided on.

She wanted her wedding to be a little different than those of her sisters, Kathy and Donna. Her gown was purchased at Up To Date in Poughkeepsie. It was modeled in a bridal magazine. On her head she planned to wear a beautiful turban made of very soft material.

I also wanted something different for my gown. I bought it at Kassell's on Broadway in Newburgh. They didn't have a bridal section. This was not considered a bride's mother's gown. It was so beautiful it was used mostly for formal affairs. Made from a very pale blue soft material, the gown was fitted, with a long cape, and the sleeves had white fur at the wrists.

Mrs. Lyndell Schaffer also wore a blue gown. She is a very beautiful woman and looked very elegant. She's a lovely person, and her husband, Richard, is very warm and friendly. It was so easy to plan different parts of the wedding with her. The reception was to be held at the Colonial Terrace in Peekskill.

The wedding day arrived, and once again my home was full of attendants. They had to get an early start because Cindy had a following photographer.

Our granddaughter Maria was the little flower girl. Her beautiful blonde hair was pulled back with a blue bow to match her gown.

I gave them two bedrooms to prepare and get dressed. Of course, Maria was with me to get ready. It worked out well, and Cindy sure made a beautiful bride along with her attendants. I could see her dad's love for her. His baby daughter was getting married.

The limos were lined outside the house as we all filed out. It was a beautiful beginning of a fall day. Driving down Bloom Street to 9W to St. Mary's Church was very familiar to my husband and me. I noticed the parking areas were filled to capacity. Guests were still going into the church. We slowly got out of the limos as the driver opened the doors.

The bridal party waited in a group until I started to walk up the steps. Mrs. Lyndell Schaffer was being escorted down the aisle to her seat. I then followed. Cindy was helped by her sisters Donna and Kathy. Kathy helped Maria to the entrance of the church. Maria carried herself so well in her long blue dress. She held a nosegay of blue and white lilies, and she followed directions to a tee as she led the bridal party down the aisle. I must say she was a little lady. She smiled as she took her small steps. She was so happy to be part of this great day. Then all the bridal party walked down and stood on the side of the front pews. The altar had two baskets of flowers on either side.

The ushers pulled the white carpet cover very carefully down the aisle as the bride prepared to walk down with her handsome dad who was dressed in his tux. As my husband walked down the aisle with our youngest daughter, it was very emotional for both of us. In her soft, high-neck, fitted, long-sleeved gown, the bride looked magnificent. She wore the gorgeous turban as her headpiece and a sheer veil over her face. It was a very different headpiece. It had some crystals in the front. As they walked slowly down the aisle, Tom gave a proud smile to the guests as the bride held firmly to his arm.

When they arrived in front of the altar, there was David, her husband-to-be, and Bobbie, the groom's brother and best man. Tom very slowly pulled the veil up and over the turban. He gave his daughter a gentle kiss, and David was there to be beside her. David was in style with his long hair. Msgr. Simmons performed a beautiful wedding ceremony. During the ceremony Cindy and David placed a beautiful white rose on Our Blessed Lady's altar. The monsignor congratulated then, and they came down the aisle as Mr. and Mrs. David Schaffer.

The limos were lined up in front of the church. The drivers waited patiently as all the guests went through the receiving line. It was a very long line, as it included nine ushers on one side and nine attendants on the other. It stretched almost to the bottom of the front steps of the church. The girls, all in blue, matched the blue sky.

As Cindy was walking down the church steps to the limo with her husband, Uncle Buster, David's uncle, said to her, "You look like an African princess." The turban had caught his eye.

We had a good hour to get to the Colonial Terrace for the reception. Within five minutes Maria fell asleep. It had been a very tiring experience for a two-and-a-half-year-old girl, but the nap worked well, as she would soon be busy taking more photographs and walking into the great reception room. It was a beautiful ride to Peekskill to get to the elegant Colonial Terrace. The building was set on a hill, and the cocktail hour was held outside with such beautiful scenery. The leaves were in the early stages of turning. There were stations displaying the different appetizers as the violins played in the background, and the rolling bars were really rolling. It was just a joyous atmosphere. It was finally time to go into the reception room. We all lined up to make our entrance, and Maria led everyone in. She walked gently down a very short flight of steps and onto the dance floor. She then took her place as the other members of the bridal party walked in.

At last the drums sounded and the other instruments began playing as Mr. and Mrs. David Schaffer's names were announced, and the couple slowly walked down the stairs hand in hand and danced to the song "Impossible" by Nat King Cole. The food was exceptional. All dinners were served, and the waitresses then brought extra platters of steak, chicken, and fish filled with side orders of shrimp.

The rolling bar was still rolling, which also included after-dinner drinks. The wedding cake was smothered in whipped cream and strawberries. As the cake was being served, another waitress brought a fancy frozen glass with vanilla ice cream and crème de menthe. As the dancing continued, I happened to check Maria's chair and saw it was empty, so I got up to check on her. At an adjoining empty table, there she was, sound asleep. Mr. Ed Porcelli was there watching her. She looked so peaceful. Ed had made her comfortable by putting the two chairs together and placing one blanket underneath her and covering her with another. She looked like an angel.

The wedding was now coming to an end, and it had been a wedding to remember. As I am writing this, I can't help thinking of what Cindy said as I was planning Kathy's wedding. She said that by the time she got married, there would not be any money left for her wedding. She knew that Donna, who was older than she was, would most likely get married ahead of her too. She ended up having the most expensive wedding.

David and Cindy took a trip to the Poconos in Pennsylvania. They were going to live in New Windsor, where David's grandfather owned a house. It was very convenient for David, as he worked for Mid Hudson Oxygen, which was owned by the Schaffer family.

Cindy had opened a nursery school, Storytime Nursery, in Marlboro at my house on Orange and Bloom. My finished basement had been turned into a lovely nursery school. She drove from Newburgh to Marlboro every morning. She was very dedicated. She also had two certified teachers who worked with her. There was only one other nursery school in Marlboro at the time, and there was always a waiting list for Cindy's school. After Cindy moved to her home on Purdy Avenue in Marlboro, her school was moved to her finished basement, which was much larger.

Tom and I at Cindy and David's wedding

THE FAMILY CONTINUES TO GROW

AFTER THIRTY-TWO YEARS IN BUSINESS, Cindy decided to retire and enjoy her granddaughters. David and Cindy have two children, Elizabeth and Matthew. She now subs in the Marlboro Elementary School.

Elizabeth is their firstborn. I remember her birth and looking at her in the nursery through the glass window at Vassar Brothers Hospital. The Schaffer grandmother, Lyndell, said she didn't look like a Schaffer, and I said she didn't look like an Amodeo baby either. Shortly after her birth, I described her as a beautiful pink rose bud just starting to open up. Then Grandma Schaffer said she was a Schaffer. To this day Elizabeth is a beautiful girl. Three months after Elizabeth was born, Kathy had her second daughter, Joelle Maryn. There were four years between them and Maria. Joelle and Maria had opposite coloring. Joelle had dark eyes and dark hair. She resembled my daughter Donna, who favors her dad.

Maria and Joelle's childhood personalities were very opposite too. Maria was very meek and timid and would always do what she was told. Joelle, on the other hand, did not. She always stood her ground. In one incident in high school, Joelle didn't agree with a teacher on a certain matter. She went to the office and met with the principal, Mr. Jack O'Donnell, to tell him what had taken place. Mr. O'Donnell did some explaining to Joelle but later told me about it with a grin. He was very fond of Joelle.

At last Cindy gave birth to my fifth grandchild, a second grandson, Matthew Amodeo Schaffer. My husband enjoyed the grandchildren very much. They were all different in their ways. When they were toddlers and even as they got older, my husband always played with them. They enjoyed Poppy very much.

Maria was the oldest and always acted older than her age. She was tall at the age of eleven and had beautiful long legs and always walked very straight.

Things were quite normal in 1984 with my daughters and their families. Kathy was taking college classes in New Paltz, Donna was planning her new home in Marlboro, and Cindy was busy with her nursery school.

It was August, and my grandchildren were preparing for the school year to open, shopping for school clothes and school supplies. Maria, the oldest, was entering sixth grade. During elementary school, her bus stop had been at the end of Orange Street by the Marlboro Firehouse. Now that she was entering the middle school, her bus stop was at the top of Hudson Terrace. One day, Maria was going by my home with a small clock. I asked her where she was going, and she answered, "MeMa, I am checking the time to see how long it will take me to walk from my house to the bus stop." The walk was from the end of Orange Street to the top of Bloom Street. On her way back, she said it took her approximately eight minutes. She would always allow extra time to get to her bus stop.

After school, Maria would always stop at my house because her mother was taking courses at SUNY New Paltz. She would have a snack and start her homework. When report cards came out, we learned that Maria had made the high honor roll. The following week as I was reading the local newspaper, I noticed a listing of the students who had made the high honor roll and saw that Maria's name had been omitted. I called up the guidance office at the middle school, and when Mary Brink answered the phone, I told her that Maria Ronk's name had been omitted. She checked her list and told me that she was very sorry, and it would be in the following week of December 17, 1984.

On December 17, Maria stopped in after school as she always did. That evening the religion class was having their Christmas party at St. Mary's Hall. I told her it would be a good idea to get her homework done before going to the party. She sat at the snack bar in my kitchen doing her homework, with her long blonde hair touching the surface of the snack bar as she wrote. Soon, she had all her homework done.

Out of the clear blue sky, she said to me, "You know, MeMa, before leaving the house to go to school, my mommy was taking a shower, and Daddy went to work. I decided to try to find some of the presents that Mom bought me for Christmas. I know she did quite a bit of shopping. I didn't see anything in her closet or the hall closet, so I decided to go to the basement. I walked down the stairs without making a sound. In the corner where the furnace is, I saw many bags. I didn't have much time, so I just looked in the first bag. As I opened it, there were all kinds of clothes for my Cabbage Patch doll. I closed the bag fast and tiptoed upstairs. MeMa, I was so happy, as I like to dress my Cabbage Patch Doll. I've had the doll for a while, and I need new clothes. MeMa, I know there's plenty of other presents, but I will open them on Christmas day."

It was about five o'clock, and I was making beef noodle soup. I suggested that Maria call her mother as her mother had just gone by my house. I asked her to tell her mother that she was going to have dinner with us, and I would bring her to St. Mary's Hall for the Christmas party.

Family photo

THE TRAGEDY THAT CHANGED MY LIFE FOREVER

THAT SAME DAY, MARIA'S DAD was home sick with a very severe cold. He told me that Kathy had called Maria's religion teacher to tell her she had some late classes in New Paltz. The teacher, Molly Gucciardo, had said she would be happy to take Maria home. Although it was just a short distance to her home, it was not safe for Maria to walk home. So I dropped Maria off at the hall for her party and then returned to my house. Maria loved Christmas and celebrated to the fullest.

The Ronks lived at the end of Orange Street, which was a dead end, and Vinnie, Donna, and Tommy were living with us at the time, as they were in the process of having their home built. That evening Tom and I spent time watching TV together with Donna and Tommy. Vinnie was not home from his job, which was in New Jersey. We were also enjoying the beautiful tree, and on my coffee table I had the nativity set on display, and the glow of the Christmas tree reflected off the pieces. It was getting late, and Tom and I decided to go to bed. By this time, Tommy was already in bed. Donna waited up for Vinnie to come home.

Having gone to sleep, I was suddenly awakened by the fire siren, and it seemed like the fire trucks were very close. As I lay on my back, I saw red flashes on my bedroom ceiling and realized that the fire trucks were going down my road. I jumped out of bed and went to the picture window in the kitchen. I saw Kathy's house down the street, and it was up in flames. In a loud, frightened voice, I called out, "Tom, it's Kathy's house!" I threw a housecoat on over my nightclothes and started to run toward the house. I found myself between a fire truck and another emergency car from the fire department.

When I reached the house, the neighbors were outside, and I asked, "Where are the girls?" They told me that Joelle was in the neighbor's house. I ran inside and asked Joelle, "Where is Maria?" She said that she was in the house. I knew in my heart that Maria was gone. At that moment, part of my life was also gone.

I left the neighbor's house with the most horrible feeling anyone could endure. I walked to my house feeling so defeated. The thought of my beautiful Maria being in that flaming house was unfathomable. (In writing this, I have to stop at this moment to get myself together for it is very painful and emotional. Yes, my heart is broken. It's very hard to relive this evening without feeling so much pain.)

I arrived at my house and walked in to find Tom in his recliner. He was holding his head in his hands and praying, "Jesus, Jesus." Vinnie had just gotten home from New Jersey when all this happened. Donna and Cindy and their husbands were all down at the burning house.

I was told that Maria's dad, Gordon, knew the room she was in and started to go through the window with the hose himself but was stopped by the firemen. They said there was no chance he'd survive. The ambulance was on the scene. Gordon had saved one daughter, Joelle, but was unable to get back in. Father Ed Dugan stopped in our home to tell Tom and me that Maria had been pulled out by firemen and placed in the ambulance with a slight pulse, along with her dad, who had burns on his arms and face. He had also suffered smoke inhalation, as had Joelle, who was also taken to the hospital.

In the meantime, Kathy was heading home and noticed all the cars at my house and people standing outside. Her first thought was that my husband or I had had a heart attack. When she got out of the car, she was told, by her cousin Bobbie, that Maria had been taken to the hospital in very serious condition. Reports were very grim; it didn't seem that Maria would make it. Kathy's screams went through me as I sat with my husband trying to figure out this nightmare.

Kathy rushed to the hospital with her sisters and their husbands. Her great-aunts Millie and Fannie were also there to comfort Kathy. Maria was pronounced dead when she got there. I can't believe that I am writing this part of my book on December 18, 2010, on the twenty-sixth anniversary of Maria's death.

Gordon and Joelle were kept overnight and released the following day. Neighbors from Orchard Street had placed a call when they saw smoke coming from the house. But the call hadn't gone through. As reported in the newspaper, AT&T and the fire control headquarters had known about the malfunction of the telephone system. How had the fire started? On the south side of the living room, an Advent wreath had been placed on a small table that held three purple candles and one rose-colored candle. Each night the family would light a candle and say a prayer. That night a rose-colored candle had been lit, as the two purple ones had been lit the two weeks before. It was up to the last person to put out the candle before bedtime. The Christmas tree was in front of the picture window, facing east.

Gordon, who was sick from a very bad cold and on medication, fell asleep in the family room while watching TV; Joelle had already fallen asleep in her mom's bed. Maria then got home from her church Christmas party. Molly Gucciardo, who drove Maria home, told her how beautiful her tree looked, and in response Maria said that her parents had wanted it in the family room, in the rear of the house. But Maria had wanted it to be visible from the road so the neighbors could see it. As you can see, Maria had won out.

Maria usually would lie down by her father and watch TV, but that night she went directly to her bedroom to sleep because she was so excited about a beautiful pillow that I had given her and she told me that she couldn't wait to use it. The pillow had been bought for me, but it was too full and too soft, and I didn't like it. She said that was the kind of pillow she liked. She also liked the cover whose pattern was small blue butterflies. Kathy was set to come home late from class that evening because one of her classmates needed a ride home to Cornwall. Remember, the last one home was to blow out the candles on the Advent wreath. I believe that for some reason the candle was too close to the curtain, and its flame ignited the wall to the Christmas tree. (The firemen's statement said that it was electrical.) Maria's teacher came to speak to me the next morning with great sadness. She told me that at the party the children all had taken turns to read the scripture. Maria had read Isaiah 9:1—"The people who walk in darkness / have seen a great light."

As Gordon described the night, he woke up to total darkness and heard a crackling noise and saw thick smoke all around. He crawled to the bedrooms, screaming out, "Maria! Joelle!" He was able to get seven-year-old Joelle out of her bed. He opened the cellar door and put her down on the stairs and was continuing to scream for Maria when Joelle came back up the stairs and had to be taken outside. He then was unable to get back in. Of all the tragedies that I had gone through in my life, this was the worst, and it still is. Kathy was under a doctor's care and later ended up having a nervous breakdown. Joelle missed her sister, and Gordon was a changed person. The entire family was never the same without our beautiful Maria here on earth with us.

It was time to make the funeral arrangements. I picked out a beautiful white casket with the help of my daughters. She was dressed in a beautiful white dress with an organdy top and velveteen bottom. She had on white leotards and slippers. These items were purchased by Aunt Fannie and Aunt Julie Amodeo.

Maria looked like an angel. At the funeral, Kathy stood at her side, and Gordon stood next to her, with white ointment on his face and hands covering the burns that he had sustained during the fire. As we were sitting there, Barbara Felicello walked in with a Cabbage Patch doll to be put in the casket. Many of Kathy and Gordon's classmates attended the wake and the funeral.

Msgr. Dugan officiated at the funeral mass along with ten other clergymen from all different denominations. Cardinal O'Connor sent a beautiful letter to the Ronk family. There were many floral pieces and mass cards (which I still have) and monetary gifts. The funeral was on December 20, 1984. It was very sad to say good-bye to Maria. My husband sobbed uncontrollably, and I told Maria, "I'm sorry I wasn't there for you," as I knew I would never see her on this earth. We all got in our limos and followed Maria to her resting place on earth, but we knew she would be an angel in Heaven. I remember Jean DeSantis telling me that they had another angel at baby Jesus's birth that year. The grave was bare initially but not for long. A marble angel was ordered from Italy. It was the same height as Maria, and it stood on a marble pedestal. Her hands were folded together, and she had flowing shoulder-length hair like Maria's. I remember Sisters Mary and Elena telling me how the angel resembled Maria. She will never be forgotten. I continue to have masses said in her honor at the anniversary of her death and on her birthday.

Kathy and Gordon have plots next to Maria, and Tom and I are head to head with her plot. In 1985 I had a beautiful nativity scene placed in front of the altar at St. Mary's. It is a single piece with Our

Lady and St. Joseph looking at our baby Jesus as He lies in the center. It is in memory of my granddaughter, Maria Ronk, taken from us before Christmas, which was the special holy day that she loved so much.

Gordon, Kathy, and Joelle lived in Middle Hope with Gordon's parents until a new house was built on the same property. Lou Quick was the builder. Sister Elena, Sister Mary, Janet Quick, Martha Giamettei, and Fran Fremgen helped with the curtains and arranged the new furniture once the house was built.

The first time that Gordon came to visit me with Joelle was a heartbreaker. There were many more sad days ahead. Bus #77 was Maria's bus, and seeing it would be another reminder that my angel was no longer here. It was a sad winter. I helped with the many thank-you notes.

Our Saturday night dinners stopped, and our vacations ended. Attending daily mass and Sunday masses and praying were the answers to our grief. When spring came, Elizabeth, Cindy's daughter, and Joelle went to a classmate's birthday party. When they came to my house after the party, they each had a balloon and said, "MeMa, we are sending these balloons to Maria in Heaven." The girls released the balloons, and we watched as they flew higher into the most beautiful blue sky. It was very touching but also heartbreaking.

Kathy was still very ill and was under the doctor's care for months. The doctors said she needed to get involved in something to help her get out of her depression. So she started her own drama program and produced many plays under the name Amodeo Productions in 1985. She still continues to work with her program called Kids on Stage.

In 1985 Mrs. James Festa, who had been Maria's fifth-grade teacher in 1983-84, called to tell me that a scholarship would be given every year at the moving-up ceremony at Marlboro Intermediate School. The following criteria are looked for in a deserving student:

Compassion	Cooperative
Sensitivity	Respectable
Helps the Less Fortunate	Independent
Conscientious	

These characteristics reflect Maria's character. Mrs. Festa told me that names of students who won the award would be added to a plaque displayed in the lobby of the school, and a check would be awarded.

In 1985, Mr. David Conn gave the first Humanitarian Award. Since 1986, this award has been given on moving-up day by me, Maria's grandmother. I made a promise to myself that as long as I am able to walk on the stage, I will present this award. It has been a great honor for me to present the award. The next one will be presented in June 2012.

All of my other grandchildren are in school. This tragedy changed our life in many ways. The holidays were always sad without Maria's presence. I would meet many of her classmates as they got older, and I would say, "I wonder what Maria would be doing at this age."

One of her classmates, Kristin Jackson whom I see quite often, is married to my great-nephew DJ. Kristin attended Maria's last birthday party that year of the house fire. They have three beautiful children, and I can't help but compare Maria with Kristen.

The marble angel that marks Maria's grave

The nativity set that we donated in memory of
Maria Ronk at St. Mary's Church

Arizona

IN 1985, MY HUSBAND WAS rushed to the hospital at three o'clock in the morning, unable to breathe. He was diagnosed with COPD, a disease of the lungs. He was confined to the hospital very often with pneumonia. The doctor felt that he should spend his winters in a dry and warm climate. He retired at sixty-two, and we thought Arizona would be the place for us to look for a winter home. My friends Gaye and Anne Goodfriend were already spending their winters there. Gaye invited us to visit her in Mesa that winter, which we did. The weather was just beautiful, and we spent two weeks there. She lived in an adult community with a swimming pool, recreation room, and other activities. Tom would use the pool, lie in that dry Arizona sun, and ride his bike around the court. I would join him. I couldn't believe how healthy he looked with a beautiful tan.

There was a beautiful corner lot located behind Gaye's property that had a roomy modular on it. It was for sale, as the occupants were up in years and were going back to Iowa to be near their children. They had been living there all year round. It had a large living room and bedroom and a small kitchen and bathroom. There was plenty of closet space in the bedroom and a nice front porch. One of the most important features of all was the central air conditioning for the hot days.

I just wasn't ready to buy a place and be away from the family during the winter months, though. After going back and forth about buying this place, I decided it was beneficial for my husband's health. I left a deposit and took care of things when I got home. He was deserving of it. The city of Mesa was located about twenty minutes from Scottsdale. Scottsdale was known as a unique place for shopping, many golf courses, and restaurants. The Sky Harbor Airport in Phoenix was about a half-hour from Mesa.

I couldn't believe we were making this great move. In August of that year, Howard and Gaye were taking a trip with his van throughout the western states and invited us to go along. Howard suggested I take some articles for our new place in Mesa. I carted some lamps and an end table, as the place was already furnished. It was a long trip. We did stop a couple of times to get a good night's sleep.

Mesa was sure hot—not a place for the summer. We spent the night there and left the next day and went sightseeing, including a stop at the Grand Canyon. Sedona, which is approximately two hours from Mesa, was interesting to see. I was impressed by how a beautiful chapel was carved in this spectacular red mountain. It was a beautiful trip home.

The following winter was our first winter away from home. We spent Christmas and New Year's with the family and left on January 3. We would always return home for Palm Sunday to spend it with the family. We never missed Easter with the family except one year in the early 1970s. That year, Fannie, John, Gaye, Howard, Tom, and I were in Rome and spent our Easter at the Vatican, with the Pope saying the mass.

We enjoyed our winters in Mesa. My husband was doing great with his COPD, and it seemed under control. Where we lived in Mesa was so convenient. The church and grocery stores were within walking distance.

My daughters and their families visited during school break. It was so nice to see them. They enjoyed their visits very much, and they were most happy with their father's health. As the years went by, the grandchildren started graduating from high school and making plans for college.

When we returned home from Arizona in the spring, we would clean around the house and get rid of the leaves that had been left behind. We'd then go back to our daily routine. We attended daily mass at St. Mary's. What better way to start the day than to hear a beautiful homily by Father Bader and to receive the Eucharist? We then would come home and have breakfast and finish our cup of coffee in the living room while watching the news. Tom and I always enjoyed being together. We would go grocery shopping and sometimes have lunch out.

On Sunday we would be invited to the home of one of our daughters for dinner. Our grandchildren would talk about what was happening in school. It was always a family gathering.

Some evenings, Tom would play bocce at the bocce court at St. Mary's. There were different groups that took part. Every Thursday was poker night at the Giuntas' house on Purdy Avenue. Every other night, he was home, and at 8:00 p.m. we would watch Bill O'Reilly on FOX News. Tom felt that the news was fair and balanced as advertised.

My Trip to Medjugorje, Yugoslavia

In 1990, six years after Maria's death, my friend Gaye told me that there was a trip to Medjugorje, Yugoslavia, where our Blessed Mother was appearing. She asked me if I would be interested, and without giving it a thought, I said yes. Of course I spoke to my husband about it, and he was in favor of my going. There were only two seats left, which Gaye and I filled.

A friend who was taking Gaye and me to Kennedy airport arrived to pick us up at 2:00 p.m. the day of our flight, and before departing, I exchanged kisses and hugs with my husband and daughters. At 3:00, it was time for my Divine Mercy Prayer, so I asked if I could have a little time of silence until I finished the prayer. I knew that my husband would be sitting at home saying the same prayer.

At 3:10 p.m., as he was saying the prayer, Tom heard a loud crash. He jumped up and ran toward the commotion at the front entrance to our home. A large car had lost control on Orange and Blooms Streets and hit our Magnolia tree and continued on to the front porch. There was $20,000 in damage. The entrance walls, which are plaster, were cracked; the kitchen cabinets were all dislocated; and many bricks on the outside of our home were broken. I was not aware until I got home. An hour before the crash, we'd been sitting out on the porch waiting for my ride to Kennedy airport.

The trip was in May, which was such a beautiful month. Our Lady was honored with many processions, and a crown of roses was placed on her head. She appeared to six children. The Communists arrested these children and the priest of St. James Church, Father Yozo. They were each interviewed separately by the Communist leader. They were asked the same questions about when they had first seen the Lady. All the answers were the same. At the time of their arrest they were hiding in St. James Church's choir loft. After their interviews, the children were released, but Father Yozo was kept in jail for eighteen months. There was a big protest to release him. He was to serve three years of hard labor. The visionaries continued meeting with all those that made this pilgrimage.

We arrived at Dubrovnik airport early in the morning and were met by a large van. We were to stay with a couple and their family in their home, and we had already paid for our room and board before leaving home.

At just the thought of visiting Medjugorje, where Our Lady was appearing, I felt this great excitement come over me. I was full of joy. I know the Holy Spirit took me over completely. As we drove along the Adriatic Sea, we could see Italy across it. The scene was awesome.

One of the passengers in the van wanted to stop and walk along the coastline and take pictures, but I honestly didn't agree. I said I had made this trip to get to Medjugorje and not to waste any time. I couldn't help myself; I just wanted to be where Our Lady was appearing. He took a few pictures, but then we left. We arrived at the home at which we were supposed to stay. As the van went up the narrow driveway, this beautiful girl came out with her sister and parents.

The driver of the van, who spoke English, introduced us to the family. The first one introduced to me was a beautiful, blue-eyed, blonde-haired girl named Maria. I immediately asked how old she was. The driver related the question to her, and she said eleven. My Maria who had died in the house fire had the same coloring, name, and age. I gave her such a big hug and imagined she was my Maria. Her sister's name was Kathy, which was my Maria's mother's name. Was this a coincidence, or did Our Lady want me to know that Maria was fine? The following day, Maria had on a lavender dress—yes, Maria's favorite color. She was running through the field with her long blonde hair blowing in the breeze. It sure was a beautiful picture. Maria had been gone for six years at this time, but I still had this hole in my heart. This day sure helped me to believe that Maria was very happy and that Our Lady wanted me to witness this beautiful scene that she had planned for me to see.

Maria's parents were wonderful, and their hospitality was just great. Most of the food we were served, they had raised themselves. The mother, who was Croatian, was an excellent cook. The father sometimes traveled to Germany, which was his birthplace. He worked in a car factory. Their daughter Kathy was very quiet and shy. She resembled her mom and Maria her dad.

After a good night's sleep and a hardy and delicious breakfast, we went to church. As we sat outside, waiting for the English mass to begin, I made myself comfortable on a bench on the side of the church. I said the Joyful Mysteries, fingering the rosary beads as I looked at the mountain where Our Lady had appeared. When I finished, I took out my little rosary purse and held the beads straight to put them gently away and couldn't believe my eyes. The links of my rosary were no longer silver but the color of gold. Before leaving the United States to make the trip to Medjugorje, I had read about this happening to some people. Yes, my Lady was right with me and wanted me to know.

I spoke to one of the priests there and told him what had happened. He told me it was something special from Our Lady. It reassured me that Maria was very happy, and Our Lady wanted me to know this.

We spent much time with the visionaries, learning about the messages they received from Our Lady. One evening we were told that Our Lady would be appearing on Apparition Hill. It was very dark and quiet when she appeared. She spoke to the visionaries, of course. We didn't hear the message. What we did see was, when she left, a big long light in the sky that went toward Mt. Kricveck, where a huge concrete cross had been built in 1933. Thirty-three was for the number of years that Jesus lived on earth.

There was no electricity on the hill where the cross was lit. What a beautiful sight. This hill was very hard to climb because it was very steep and rocky, but I made it with much care. It was a beautiful place to meditate.

The time finally came when I had to depart. What a spiritual trip it had been for me—I returned again in 1991. I sent gifts to the Barack family when I returned but was informed that the gifts were opened by the Communists. I was told by a chaperone from Pennsylvania who made many flights to Medjugorje that the Communists went through the packages and often took their contents. She told me about ten years ago that Maria had married and had children.

162

I feel that the evil one tried to disrupt this beautiful spiritual trip I had planned. He didn't succeed. When I got home and was told and saw the damage, I said, "It could be fixed." My husband was upset for me and was surprised by my reaction. I was so full of the Holy Spirit and wouldn't let this problem spoil my beautiful trip.

THE ACCIDENT

Our first grandson, Thomas Amodeo Porcelli, was born in Monticello, N.Y. The family later moved to Marlboro where he attended the Marlboro schools. He graduated from Marlboro High School.

He enjoyed playing high school football and was an outstanding player. He loves to travel and has made three trips abroad. He works at the Marlboro High School and enjoys working with the students.

My granddaughter Elizabeth had graduated from high school and had continued her education at Dutchess Community College and Quinnipiac in Connecticut. She double-majored in journalism and media arts and graduated summa cum laude.

She worked in New York City, Connecticut, and Houston, Texas. She is now employed by a private equity firm in Houston. She is married to Bob Henry and has two beautiful children, Beau and Healey. In August 2011 I visited and enjoyed myself with their family and their two dogs. I enjoyed their back porch with the TV and a glass of wine. I met many of her friends, and I must say she is lucky to have them around her. Her husband, Bob, is a Southern gentleman.

Joelle graduated from PACE University in New York City. She loved to sing, and in high school she participated in many musical productions. Joelle started taking voice lessons at the age of fifteen. She continued while attending college and added acting classes. She performed at Windows on the World and the Supper Club. She was also a VJ on a major network. In college she met Brian Hannabery, who was from Pennsylvania. Brian was an IT major while Joelle was in communications. They dated for a couple of years and then married.

They lived in New York and then moved to California. Brian is a computer engineer. While in California, Joelle was in real estate. She did very well. Real estate was at its peak at that time. Her husband was then transferred to Austin, Texas. They sold their home in California and purchased another one in Austin. They have two beautiful children, Siena and Blake Thomas. In 2008, Joelle started her own cosmetic company, CATTIVA (which means "naughty" in Italian). She works very hard, and her company is now nationwide and doing very well. Brian works from home and is always at his computer. He also helps Joelle with the packaging of the CATTIVA makeup. In 2010 Joelle was chosen as Mrs. Austin. The pageant was held on March 3, and I attended. It was very exciting.

Our grandson Matthew was the last to graduate from high school. He enrolled in Norwich University in Vermont, graduated with honors, and joined the army. He was stationed in Fort Gordon, Georgia, and married his high school sweetheart, Amy Slader. She's a beautiful girl with a beautiful voice and is a talented artist. After five months at Camp Gordon, he was given a furlough before his deployment to Iraq with the 501st Signal Battalion.

I remember we assembled at his mom's home before he had to leave to go back to Fort Gordon. Deacon Vincent Porcelli (his uncle) led us in prayer. It was quite early in the morning, and the sky was still gray. My heart was saddened, and it sure matched the gray sky. I wondered, will the Lord bring our Matthew back? I kissed him long and then went to the back bedroom to watch him leave. As I pushed the curtain aside, he got in his dad's car and left.

The fighting in Iraq was very heavy, and we were losing a lot of our men, and many were wounded. After a year in Iraq, he came home. He was met by his wife and daughter, Morgan, and his parents in Fort Campbell, Kentucky. He came to visit the family in Marlboro. We were so delighted and thankful that he had come home safely. After spending sixteen months in the States, he was deployed to Iraq for a second tour, but not before he was given a furlough. He spent some more time with us in Marlboro with a larger family.

He was to leave on December 28, 2004, to go back to his base, and he was set to leave shortly after that date for Iraq.

I promised Mathew that I would prepare an Italian dish before he left. One of his favorites was pasta fagioli. I told him that I would bring it up at twelve noon. At 11:55, I told Tom that I was going to take lunch to Matthew. Tom said he wasn't feeling too well. I told him I would run it up and that we would have our lunch when I got back. I encouraged him to rest, but instead he decided to come with me so he could say good-bye to Matthew. He realized that he wouldn't see his grandson for a long time.

Tom put on his red jacket, and we walked out together to get into the car. Tom sat in the passenger seat in the front, and I placed the covered stainless pot with the steaming pasta fagioli on the floor of the car by Tom's feet. I slowly went down Bloom Street to make sure the pot would stay in place. After I made the left turn by the Marlboro Free Library, I began carefully driving through town on 9W. It was a mild day, and things were normal until we passed the gas pumps at the Getty station, which is when I heard a loud bang and felt the impact. My car had been struck. I heard my husband shout, "Oh!" and the windshield shattered. I realized he had hit the windshield with his head. The young fellow who had hit us came to the door and opened it and said how sorry he was. My husband just sat there and never said a word.

When the twenty-three-year-old driver of the car that hit us was questioned by the police chief, it was found that he had a suspended license and drugs in his car. He was arrested. After we were hit, a gentleman came to the car and said that he had followed the car that hit us from Highland and it had been speeding. He said there was nothing that I could have done. Michele Giametta, my niece, was driving north on 9W and noticed the gray Lincoln and knew it was our car. The police were stopping traffic at that time, so she ran down. I asked her to sit in the car and hold Tom's hand so I could call my daughter Cindy. Cindy came down from Purdy Avenue with her son Matthew, who was to be leaving for Iraq in a couple of hours. The policeman, Mr. Lofaro, started to make out his report. He stated that Tom wasn't wearing a seatbelt but indicated he wasn't injured. How could he not be injured when his head hit the windshield and shattered it and he was unresponsive? My chest hit the steering wheel, and I had my seatbelt on. The ambulance did not rush. When it got there, two attendants put Tom in the ambulance, and I went along.

As the ambulance drove down 9W, my husband started to talk and said he was swallowing blood and couldn't breathe. I begged them to please hurry, as they seemed to be going very slow. I never did see such unprofessional attendants take care of a very sick man. They were young and not very experienced.

When we got to the ER, Cindy, David, Lyndell and Richard Schaffer, and my sister Millie and her son Chuck were waiting. Tom was wheeled into one room and I into another. My chest was totally black and blue, and I was in pain. I knew my injury was from my chest hitting the steering wheel. Since I'd had a stent placed in my artery at the beginning of the year, I had to be x-rayed to see if any damage had been done.

I didn't know the extent of my husband's injury until the nurse came in to tell me that my husband's condition was very serious and that he would have to be transported to St. Francis Hospital in Poughkeepsie, where they had a special unit for head trauma. The nurse wheeled him into my room before they took him to be transported. When they wheeled him in, I couldn't see him, as his head and face were bandaged. I couldn't say a word, and I don't believe he knew what was going on.

On his way to St. Francis, he went into cardiac arrest and had to be brought back. Thank God there was a different team on this ambulance. He was rushed to St. Francis, where a different team of doctors was waiting. He was put on life support and given the last rites of the Catholic Church. My sister-in-law, Fannie Amodeo, was there with her husband John and son Anthony, awaiting Tom's arrival. However, he was already there, and they didn't recognize him. His head and face had become very swollen, and he was completely bandaged.

I was still at St. Luke's with Lyn Schaffer and Julie Amodeo. I requested that I be released so I could be with my husband. I was taken home first. Fannie and Joyce Amodeo had left St. Francis so they could let me know what was going on. I insisted that I wanted to go to St. Francis to be with Tom. Lyn and Richard took me there, where I met Cindy, David, and my sister Millie. I was told by the attending doctors to gather the family together. My grandson Matthew put in a call to his commanding officer and explained what was taking place, and he was allowed an extension.

My daughter Donna and her husband were in Florida and were scheduled to leave the next day for a cruise. They left for the hospital immediately and got there in the wee hours of the morning. They arrived with Joe and Linda DeMarco, who were supposed to go on the cruise with them. Kathy was home at the time but had been told it wasn't a serious accident. She immediately came over to the hospital. Joelle came in from California and Elizabeth from Texas.

My husband had a pacemaker and was on the blood thinner Coumadin. The doctor had often reminded him that a fall or injury to the head could be very serious. In addition to his head injury, he had broken ribs and collar bone and injuries to his heart and lungs.

When I was riding to St. Francis with Lyn and Richard Schaffer, my life felt so dark. As we rode on 9W, I felt then and there that my wonderful life with Tom would end. When I arrived in his room, he was in an induced coma. There were tubes and wires connecting machines to all parts of his body. My daughters and my nieces Patty Pascale and Anne Marie stayed all night and many nights after that.

Two days after the accident, I wasn't feeling too well. I had chest pains. My son-in-law Vinnie took me to my primary doctor, Dr. George Profeta in Newburgh. My chest was still very bruised from hitting the steering wheel. The doctor ordered an x-ray. My blood pressure was 200 over 100. He became very concerned and wanted me to be admitted to the hospital, but I refused. He gave me Norvasc for the blood pressure. I did have an x-ray taken, and the stent in the artery of my heart had not been disturbed.

Vinnie and I left for the trip back to St. Francis. We walked to the waiting room where all my family had settled. When I entered, Joelle approached me and said, "Grandma, Poppy is off the life support." I could feel myself passing out. I was so overwhelmed with joy. I couldn't wait to see him. As I was going to his room, a nurse told me that they'd had to put him back on the life support. What a disappointment that was.

Every day, it was the same story. The heart doctor would come in and speak to me and tell me that Tom's heart wasn't healing. I would get the same news from the next doctor regarding his lungs. His brain remained swollen. At that point I knew there was someone higher than these doctors. I realized the doctors didn't want me to get my hopes up and were doing their best to help Tom.

A great consolation to me was seeing our godson Glenn Paulsen arrive at the hospital in the morning before my daughters and me. He would stop with coffee and bagels before going to work at IBM. He would always accompany me to Tom's ICU room for support when Tom was on life support.

Every day, I would go into his room and try to read the amount of oxygen he was on, and it was always different. I was told that usually after ten days, they took the patient off life support and performed a tracheotomy. The lung doctor told me that he would have to go to a nursing home. After two weeks he left St. Francis and went to Wingate at Ulster.

Prior to his release from St. Francis, his lung doctor told me that if he made it, he would be on life support or oxygen for the rest of this life. That didn't sit well with me. I was devastated and refused to accept it. What I did instead was pray my daily rosary with the special pair of beads that I'd brought with me to Medjugorje, Yugoslavia, where our Blessed Mother had appeared.

Wasn't this an appropriate time to use them? Every day, I would put these rosary beads over my husband's heart, lungs, head, and broken wrists as I prayed and as he just lay there. Yes, physically he was out of it, but not spiritually. He was on the bottom floor of Wingate, where his breathing was monitored. I continued with my rosary and added a large beautiful picture of the Sacred Heart on the wall facing him. I didn't miss a day. I was at his side from the first day of the accident. The doctor and nurses were concerned about me, as I had lost ten pounds and had a difficult time sleeping. After ten days in that room, he was transferred to another room, which meant he was slightly improving.

One afternoon when he was napping, I decided to get a snack. When I returned and entered the room, there was our niece, Joyce Amodeo, sitting at his bedside, rubbing his hand and whispering to him. It was a picture of love and caring. He was fond of her and her daughters. He saw a lot of Katie and Emily, Joyce and Johnnie's twins. They are very sweet girls.

One night after I visited Tom, I found that my niece Debbie Adamschick had prepared a delicious dinner for me and left it with Joyce, who lived next door to me. As soon as I arrived home, Joyce was there with this tasty dish, and it was really great. This then happened quite frequently. God bless her.

I was very tired that night and went to bed about nine o'clock. At eleven o'clock that night, the phone rang. When I answered it, I heard the person say, "Wingate at Ulster." My heart dropped—something bad must have happened to my Tom. The nurse said, "Your husband wants to speak to you." At this time he was in a wheelchair, and he had gone to the nurses' station.

"Hi," I said.

And the lovely voice said to me, "I just wanted to tell you I love you."

"I love you," I replied.

The nurses seemed amused. I could hear them in the background. They realized the love he had for me. The nurse told me that he wouldn't go to bed until they dialed my number. They realized it was rather late to call me, she said, but he had insisted. It was a very happy call, and I slept in peace the rest of the night and thanked God! This was a great change from the first week that he had been there. He had fallen out of bed and hit the radiator with his back. He lay there quite a while before he was put back into bed. After this incident, I'd hired a nurse to be at his bedside for the fear that he would fall again and break a hip. The doctors told me it would be the end if that happened. He deserved the best of care.

I could see big improvements in him. But he wasn't able to swallow yet, so a feeding tube was inserted in his stomach at St. Francis. He was transferred by ambulance to have this procedure done. At Wingate the nurse would thicken any liquid given to him. I had to practice this until he was ready to come home.

Tom's Second Homecoming

DID I SAY "COME HOME"? Yes, he would be coming home on February 13, after spending two weeks in St. Francis and four weeks at Wingate. There are no words in the dictionary or anywhere else to convey the feeling I had in my heart knowing that my Tom, my love, was finally coming home.

To me this was a miracle! The doctors had never given me hope. I believe that in my joy I kissed him more than I had in all our previous fifty-seven-and-a-half years of marriage. We had been given another chance. Thank you, Jesus. Thanks to our Sacred Heart and our Lady of Medjugorje for bringing my husband home to me. One nurse said to me, "I see your prayers were answered." I'd never given up.

The day he was to come home, Vinnie, Donna, and I went to Wingate. I don't remember seeing a more beautiful day driving on 9W; everything around me was glowing. The road had seemed different to me for the past six weeks. I'd had a heavy heart, and all the days were dark. The days of going on and getting off the elevators at St. Francis and Wingate were full of doubt and fear. But on February 13, the elevators were filled with joy. When I got off, I didn't have a knot in my stomach; even the nurses' station looked joyous. We walked into his room, and there was Tom, sitting in a chair. He was all dressed up; one of the nurse's aids had helped him to dress. He looked quite thin in his white shirt, navy pants, and heavy red winter jacket. But he was still the handsome man I'd married. As he left the staff at Wingate, they wished him the best of health.

Vinnie parked at the front entrance of the red brick Wingate building. He opened the door, and Tom got out of the wheelchair and into the front seat while Donna and I sat in the back. He seemed rather quiet until we got into Marlboro.

Vinnie stopped at the gas station, and Tom's brother John and nephews Johnnie-Boy and Steven came out to welcome him home. Then we left and continued our trip home.

Kathy and Cindy were at our house waiting for our arrival. Over my kitchen door I have a small picture of the Sacred Heart. When Tom entered, the first thing he did was turn around and look at the Sacred Heart and bless himself.

As time went on, he seemed somewhat confused. He remembered his home in Italy, in Monteforte in the province of Avellino, and got it confused with his home in Marlboro, where he'd lived since 1956. Vinnie took Tom's red jacket off him and helped him to get into a more comfortable pair of pants and shirt. In the meantime I made chicken soup and removed the vegetables and just added pastina to the broth. I had thickened it slightly with milk. I fed him because he hadn't fed himself in six weeks. He ate very slowly and drank the milk very slowly. I was a nervous wreck. Vinnie and the girls spent the day with us. That evening he retired to bed early.

It took him a week to get used to his home and surroundings. His appetite was getting better, and he started to gain weight. It wasn't much longer before the feeding tube was taken out. He was starting to get back to his routine. It was during Lent that Tom and I went to daily mass in the chapel of the rectory. Father Bader came down to say the mass, and when he saw Tom, he said, "Our Easter miracle." Father had visited him in the ICU in St. Francis Hospital and knew he'd had serious injuries.

Tom had an appointment with his primary doctor, at which he was given medication for his COPD, which was under control. The following day, he had an appointment at the Heart Center with Dr. Thomas Portelli, who felt he was coming along well. Last but not least, he visited Dr. Hughes in Cornwall for he was in the beginning stages of Parkinson's. He followed the doctor's orders and was doing well.

Every day was a family affair. The girls and their husbands would always visit. Our Sunday dinner was always at one of their homes. Tom's brother Bert was very helpful to us. He would sometimes accompany us to Tom's doctor's visits. He also would sit with Tom when I had errands to run.

Enjoying Life after Tom's Hospitalization

In December 2004 my daughters decided they would give me a surprise eightieth birthday party. It was to be held at Villa Borghese in Wappinger Falls on May 6, 2005. But after the accident Tom and I were involved in, with his prognosis not good, they didn't know whether the party would take place. They were given a certain date until which they could hold the reception room. Everything was in full swing once the girls knew my husband was improving and would be coming home on February 13, 2005. I can't believe that my daughters were planning this big eightieth surprise party for me, and I never had any idea what was going on.

My husband was the most important person, and he needed my full attention. I would cook and feed him the healthiest food, take him for short walks, and make sure he took his medication. All of this was so important to make him strong. Of course an afternoon nap helped him cope the rest of the day.

He wore jogging pants during the day, as there wasn't a pair of pants that would fit him. They would fall off him. I decided to buy smaller pants that he would be able to wear. That was a lot better. His color started to improve, and so did his appetite.

One day my daughter picked up the mail and told me that we'd been invited to Mr. and Mrs. Frank Leoce's fiftieth wedding anniversary to be held at the Villa Borghese on May 6. I felt that we should make every effort to attend the occasion, as Flo is a very kind and giving person, but I told my daughters that we would attend only if their dad was up to it. It was still seven weeks away, and I expected Tom would be doing better by then.

My two granddaughters from Texas also had been invited to the party for the Leoces. They came a few days earlier, on May 3, and planned to stay for Mother's Day too. Their Poppy really enjoyed their visit.

For some reason I wasn't overjoyed to attend this celebration, as I wasn't quite over the accident and the fright that I had gone through. It had taken a toll on me. My grandchildren were going through my clothes to tell me what to wear. They picked out one of my pretty gowns. I said, "No way. It's not my celebration, but the Leoces." They didn't want to insist for fear of giving away my eightieth surprise party. So I wore a silk two-piece pantsuit, but I wasn't too happy with it, as it didn't fit properly; I'd lost some weight.

May 6 was finally upon us. I helped Tom to get dressed, and then I got ready. Tom wasn't aware of the party either because the girls were afraid that he might slip and tell me. Donna and Vinnie were to pick us up for the great surprise. As Tom sat in his recliner watching at the TV while we waited, he decided not to go. I called Donna up and told her that her dad wasn't up to going. She said, "Please put him the phone." I did as I was asked. I didn't know what the conversation was about, but after they hung up, he said, "We'd better go." I later found out what the conversation was about. Donna had told him, "Daddy, it's Mom's eightieth surprise birthday party, and you've got to go." Donna and Vinnie arrived in fifteen minutes. I noticed that Donna was upset but not for long.

It was a Friday night, and the traffic was heavy. When we arrived at the Villa Borghese, Vinnie let out Tom, Donna, and me at the front entrance. Donna ran ahead, saying she was going to the ladies' room. As Tom and I walked into the lobby, we could hear music. I looked around at the parties going on and realized I didn't know which room the Leoces' anniversary party was in. We didn't see Donna at all.

I saw a gentleman dressed in a tux, and thinking that he was the manager, I asked him, "Do you know what room the Leoce party is in?" He said no, but he would get someone to help me. A young lady came up to us to see if she could help us. She checked the listings at the podium in the lobby. We waited patiently as her fingers flipped through the pages and stopped. "There is an eightieth surprise party for Anne Amodeo," she said. I just stood there, and Tom said, "It's for you." She showed us to the room, and as I entered, a room full of guests shouted, "Surprise!" I was in shock and couldn't respond. It had indeed been a surprise until I was told by the young lady in the lobby. The place was decorated more like a wedding. It was fabulous!

The grandchildren all met me and Tom by the entrance along with my daughters. Donna had run ahead into the reception room to see the surprise on my face when I entered. It was a surprise and was wonderful to see family members, friends, and Father Bader. The food was excellent, and so was the music. The girls did a fantastic job.

Vinnie gave a special blessing and added how happy my husband was to be able to attend. Tom got a standing ovation. We did dance to a couple of slow songs. I couldn't believe we were dancing again.

As it grew late, everyone was still dancing. It was past the time to cut the cake, and Tom was getting tired. John, Tom's brother, was preparing to leave along with his wife Fannie, Debbie, and Joyce. Tom went home with them, and Debbie and Joyce stayed with Tom until I got home. It was very kind of my nieces to do this.

Tom was coming along. Fall was around the corner. Winters in Arizona had ended. We had spent sixteen winters there.

The second affair that we attended was the wedding of my great-niece Candice Amodeo. Her fiancé, Tim Jordan, was a police officer in Highland at the time. He had come to visit Tom while Tom was a patient at Wingate. I remember him going to the nurses' station and telling them, "Take good care of my uncle Tom; I want him to be at my wedding." Honestly, at that time I didn't think that he would make it, as he still wasn't out of the woods yet. Thank God he did. He was in better health for this affair than he was for my eightieth birthday. Tom and I danced to "It's Impossible," a song with beautiful lyrics made famous by Perry Como. As he held me tightly and looked at me with that haze in his beautiful green eyes, that said it all. Silently, I thanked the Lord for these beautiful moments. I knew that every day since Tom left Wingate was a special gift from God.

The wedding was in August, and it was a beautiful day, so Tom and I took a brief walk outside. The flowers were in full bloom, the grass was a beautiful shade of green, and the sky was a beautiful blue. I said to Tom three words: "It's God's creation."

He stopped a second and said to me, "You're very happy."

I responded, "Yes, I am very happy and full with spiritual joy that I am here with you."

Dr. Keith Festa was a guest at the wedding and was very happy to see Tom there. He is an administrator at St. Francis Hospital, and his family and I were neighbors for years. He was very kind to me and my family while Tom was a patient at the hospital. He spoke to Tom's doctors and tried to keep our hopes up.

It was a beautiful wedding and one I will always remember.

Tom participating in many of the veteran parades and ceremonies

A Big Change

THE YEAR 2006 CAME. TOM was improving health-wise. It wasn't a bad year; he was able to continue his short walks, visit with our daughters and their husbands, go out for lunch, and take some short rides. Tom would show us some of the roads and buildings he'd worked on when he was with Local 137. The IBM buildings, Taconic Road, and Bear Mountain were some of the spots that we visited. He had worked on these projects many years earlier, but he was very proud. Those were the years when we'd taken our trips to the Islands and Europe. That was when he was young and strong.

In March 2007, I noticed a big change in him. He had no appetite at all. I would fuss to make his smaller meals. One day I prepared dinner and set it on the table and told him it was ready. I had to go into the other room to put some clothes away. When I came back into the kitchen, I couldn't believe that his dish was completely empty. I was so thrilled for the first second, but then I realized there was no way he could have finished his dinner in that short period of time. Without saying a word, I looked into the garbage pail and picked up some newspaper, and there was his dinner. He looked at me and said, "I just can't eat." What could I say? It just broke my heart.

That following Monday, he had an appointment with his doctor. He was starting to lose some of the weight he had gained upon coming home from Wingate. I was told to give him four cans of Ensure a day and try to have him eat some food. He would eat very little. I would also make milkshakes and ice cream with peaches. Some days he would eat almost nothing.

The girls noticed that he was going downhill. He was exceptionally tired. He wasn't attending mass but did take the "real food" that I would bring to him after I attended mass. Yes, the Eucharist.

When I wasn't able to go to church, Deacon Porcelli would bring the Eucharist after Sunday mass. On the first Fridays, Fannie would bring it to Tom when I was unable to attend. We would listen to the mass on EWTN and every day at three o'clock recite the Divine Mercy Prayer. Tom was a very prayerful person, and I knew he would be in Heaven when he left this earth.

Tom was at the point where he didn't want to be left alone. I would go to CVS to pick up a prescription, and when I got home, he'd be waiting for me. He told me that he prayed from the time I left until I got home that I would be safe.

Tom had to go to his primary doctor for a checkup. Donna drove. After his checkup, the doctor told us that he would need hospice shortly. I couldn't believe my ears. I remember coming home from New Windsor as Donna drove, with Tom in the front passenger seat. We drove home on River Road, and everything in my life seemed to be coming to an end. I couldn't help myself and found tears running down my cheeks. I didn't want to believe that Tom's life was coming to an end. I realized that mine would never be the same without him.

My family stopped to see him more frequently now. My sister Millie and her husband Bob visited too, which was a good thing because Bob would go back and talk about his job with Local 825.

Tom's brother John and Fannie would stop in after Sunday mass along with many friends. He would wait for his daughters to come. Donna came at 12:15 when she got out of work, Cindy visited in the evenings, as she had her nursery school during the day, and Kathy was in and out. Father Bader came up late one morning to anoint him and chat awhile.

Tom was fading away. He drank very little Ensure, and he was getting weaker. My daughters were down one Sunday afternoon, and he was unable to stand or walk. Vinnie went to the rectory to get the wheelchair. He was unable to stand unassisted.

This was the second week in May. I kept reminding him that our sixtieth anniversary was coming on June 1, and I wanted to renew our wedding vows. I told him that he had to eat and drink the Ensure. Of course that didn't happen. Father Bader had a special mass for those who were married for twenty-five, fifty, or sixty years or more in which the couples would renew their vows.

June came, and Father Bader mentioned our names during the ceremony. He knew how badly I had wanted to be there for this occasion. We were there in spirit. That was very thoughtful of Father Bader. Thanks again to Father Bader.

That week Donna and Vinnie decided to come live in our home. It was such a big help. Vinnie would get up at night when he heard Tom, and he bathed him and dressed him. Tom needed help with all of these things now.

Tom was having trouble breathing. His COPD was at a very serious stage, and he ended up in the hospital. I called St. Mary's Rectory, and Father Bader came down and prayed over him.

His doctor came in and read the results of his breathing test and said that when he left the hospital the next day, it would be time to have hospice come to the house. I stayed overnight with him.

The next day our bedroom was set up for the equipment needed to make Tom comfortable. One machine was set at the bottom of our bed to supply Tom with the oxygen that he needed to help him breathe. Another was set up for medications. There were wires crossing the room to the electrical sockets in the wall. On the white walls of our bedroom was a small picture of the Sacred Heart, which faced Tom. Along the left wall above the dresser was a beautiful crucifix on a green velvet plaque, which we had purchased in Milan, Italy, on one of our vacations. On the left side of the bed was a large picture of the Sacred Heart with his arms extended out to welcome Tom home. Where the Son is, so is His Mother. The Immaculate Heart of Mary was on my side.

Tom lay quietly for the most part except when he would call out, "Annie, where are you?" Of course I was always there holding his hand or rubbing his head. You could always hear the oxygen machine and the air conditioning running.

I notified my granddaughters from Texas and Matthew, our grandson who was waiting to go to the State Trooper Academy, of his condition. My other grandson, Tom, lived in Marlboro.

We were told by the hospice nurse that he had about one week. I didn't leave his side. In fact he made sure I was with him at all times.

Tom's Final Homecoming

ON JUNE 18, 2007, AT 4:55 p.m., Tom went home to the Lord. My niece Anne Marie from Long Island spent the week with us. Prior to his passing, I sat on the bed alongside him, holding his hand, and I said the Divine Mercy Chaplet at three o'clock.

His breathing was very shallow, and he opened his eyes and looked at me and took his last breath. It was a very peaceful death. He was surrounded by his family and some friends.

I told everyone that I wanted some time alone with my love. They left and closed the door. I spoke to him and told him what a great husband, dad, and grandfather he had been. I held his hand and rubbed his forehead until he started growing cold. I kissed him and said we would always be together. I would always love him.

Joelle got here on time with her daughter, Siena, to see Poppy, but he was out of it. Prior to their arrival, he couldn't wait to see them. He was looking forward to seeing his great-granddaughter, Siena, but the time ran out. Elizabeth arrived here at 5:45 because her plane from Houston had been delayed. She sobbed over not getting a chance to say good-bye.

The nurse from hospice was called to make the final report of his death. There was a nurse present, but a specific nurse had to sign the death certificate. They were a fine group. Later, Carl DiDonato came to remove my husband's body. It was very sad.

The next morning, I went to DiDonato's to make the funeral arrangements with my daughters. We brought his clothes and shoes and picked out a beautiful casket. Carl DiDonato and LarryCavazza did a wonderful job. Tom had lost thirty-five pounds.

We then went to pick out our floral pieces. I picked out a beautiful heart of miniature red roses with some miniature white roses and a red ribbon with "My Love" written on it. Yes, he was my first love and always will be.

In his obituary I stated, "In lieu of flowers, please donate to the St. Mary's Renovation Fund." There were many mass cards also. We were very impressed with the generosity of our family and friends.

Tom had a beautiful farewell. He had a full military funeral, and the Knights of Columbus stood guard at the casket. It was very impressive, and the American Legion and the firemen paid their respects as well.

It was very difficult for me to say so long to the love of my life, but the memories of the life we shared together will keep him close to me forever.

The mass was very beautiful. Father Bader met the casket as it was brought into the church. Deacon Porcelli and Deacon Repke were at his side. Deacon Porcelli gave the eulogy. Barbara Roser was the organist, and Nancy Porcelli sang that day with so much emotion. The "Ave Maria" went right to our hearts. When the mass was over, the casket was turned to be led out. Tom was very familiar with where his casket was placed because we had always sat in the front row. I'm sure the Lord didn't say to Tom, "Who are you?" We followed the casket out to the hearse and then got into our limo to go to St. Mary's Cemetery. We went up Bloom Street and past our home that Tom loved. We arrived at the cemetery, and the marble statue of the Sacred Heart was waiting for Tom. It was a beautiful day. The military from West Point was waiting and gave Tom the honor he deserved. The flag was presented to me. The birds also honored him with their singing. Leaving the cemetery was very difficult. It was most difficult for me to leave Tom.

Driving home in the limo going down Lattintown Rd and Western Ave, I realized my life would be greatly changed now. As I looked out the window, even the trees seemed to be at a standstill. It was a strange feeling. Passing the post office, I thought of how Tom would always stop to get the mail after running errands. These things will pass with time, but the hole in my heart will always be there. They say time heals, but I haven't found it yet, and it will soon be five years. You go on the best you can with your life and your beautiful family. I get the most consolation from my Lord, Our Blessed Mother, and my prayer life.

The following is a note I received from a parishioner, Doris Hennekens. I was very thankful for her thoughtfulness:

Bird Song!!! You know how when something happens in our lives we associated it with something we hear or see? Well, I can't imagine how any of us could ever hear a bird sing again without thinking of your Tom.

Today at the cemetery, the birds were drowning out what Father was saying, but it didn't matter. They were singing Tom into Heaven and so many of us heard it. I said something to Donna about it and she was very aware of it, too. I remember with other deaths, that there was something we looked for—a star, a rainbow, raindrops or sunshine.

There always seems to be something to hang on to that the Holy Spirit sends us, telling us that it's all right, our beloved one is where he belongs. Tonight, while I sat on my porch reading, the birds started to sing and I thought of you and Tom and your devotion to each other. There was so much beauty in both of you that even the birds have to sing about it and I had to write and tell you about how I saw it and heard it, too.

Dear Anne and All,

I know it's not going to be easy for you. Know that you will be in our prayers as you have been for many months. I also know you have a wonderful family surrounding you and probably don't need "more people," but if you do, 236-#### is my number and we can always talk about the bird song or whatever.

With Love,
Doris

Tom and I walking on the beach

LIFE AFTER I LOST THE LOVE OF MY LIFE

My DAUGHTERS AND THEIR HUSBANDS fill much of my time with their thoughtfulness and visits. Donna and Vinnie have a beautiful vacation spot on Orchid Island in Vero Beach. I'm always invited to go. I've visited my granddaughter Elizabeth, her husband Bob, and their two children, Beau and Healy, in Houston, Texas, with Cindy and David. I visit Joelle and her husband, Brian, and their two children, Siena and Blake, with Kathy and Gordon in Austin, Texas.

Being a daily communicant starts my day. What could be better than receiving the Body and Blood of Jesus daily? I live alone, but I am not alone; I always feel the Lord's presence. Father Bader gives such meaningful homilies that I can relate to in my daily life.

I must say I feel Tom's presence with me at all times. There are many beautiful songs that I hear that we used to dance to. Tom and I just loved to dance. I still take out photos and look at them. They're from the beginning of our relationship up to the last days.

I visit his grave quite often. The grave of my granddaughter, Maria, is right behind him. My brother John and Daisy are just a stone's throw away. Tom's friend Howard is two graves down.

In 2011, on Memorial Day, Edward Murphy, a very patriotic veteran, was kind enough to place a flag holder and flag with the veteran's inscription. He cemented it on the left side of the statue of the Sacred Heart of Jesus. After completing this chore, he went to his car, put on his military hat, and saluted Tom's grave with a salute and the music of "The Star Spangled Banner." The flag he had just installed was blowing in the breeze. It really touched me. Before placing the flag stand in the ground, he had cleaned the statue of the Sacred Heart with cleaning materials he'd brought along.

Edward Murphy is patriotic in the full sense of the word. He is always in attendance at the Memorial Day program held in our school and takes an active part. He always brings me vegetables from his garden. Ed has always been there for me. God bless you, Ed, and your beautiful wife, Bernadette, who is very active in our church. Their daughters Cara and Megan and son Joseph are wonderful.

I didn't realize how much a person's life could change following the loss of a husband of sixty years. We had an acquaintance for eight years before our marriage too. I relive part of my life as I listen to many songs of the 1940s and up, especially "I'll Be Loving You Always," "Are You Lonesome Tonight?," and many other beautiful songs. After I live through the lyrics, I know I'm just dreaming.

I'm not dreaming when I say I am enjoying my daughters, their husbands, my four grandchildren, and my seven great-grandchildren. I often think of my first precious granddaughter, Maria, who perished in the house fire at age eleven on December 18, 1984. This was the most tragic thing that happened in my life. I know that she is with her Poppy in Heaven.

The early part of my life was tragic, dark, and depressing until I met my prince, who brought me sixty years of happiness.

God bless you, Tom. You have all my love. One day we will be together again in Heaven.

Our Recliners

Tom and I used to sit in recliners in our living room to watch TV. There was a small table with a lamp that divided us. At times we would have lunch in there. I would bring Tom's lunch and a glass of wine to him on his favorite tray.

We always watched the news. One of Tom's favorite shows was the Bill O'Reilly program that came on in the evening. We also enjoyed EWTN. There were many interesting programs on, and one of our favorites was at 3:00 p.m., *The Divine Mercy Chaplet*, which we never missed.

The evening after the funeral, I sat in my recliner. There was such emptiness. I couldn't stand to sit there, especially when I stared at his empty recliner. He loved that recliner so much that when the great-grandchildren came to visit, they would poke their heads in the living room to look for their Poppy when they first entered the house and didn't see him right away.

I finally realized that recliner would stay empty, and Tom would no longer be sitting there. Those recliners were more than twenty years old but were still in good condition. They were very comfortable. I decided to put them in my finished basement and order a new one from Ethan Allen, where I had purchased the original two.

I told my daughters about this, and they thought it was a good idea. After two months my beautiful white recliner arrived and was placed where my old recliner had been.

Later, when I entered the room and saw Tom's recliner was gone, I was very unhappy and sad. I felt like a traitor. I just hated going into the room. I spoke to my daughters about it, and they disagreed with me. They liked the new recliner very much. To fill Tom's place they set up a large vase with a beautiful arrangement of flowers. No way did that picture suit me.

So one day I dragged the white recliner out of the living room and positioned it in one of the corners in the dining room. I went down to the basement and opened the door to the garage and started to drag my recliner out, with the intent of putting it back in the living room. It was very heavy for me, but I struggled with it until I got it halfway up the small hill of my driveway. It was hot, and I was sweating and out of breath.

I saw my neighbor, Mr. Rounds, and asked him if he would bring the recliner in for me through the front entrance. He was very gracious. But there was still Tom's recliner to bring up from the basement. I called my grandson Tommy. I wanted him to bring the other recliner up, but I was unable to reach him.

I then called my grandson Matthew, and he came right down. He carried the chair through the front door and into the living room and placed it next to the other recliner. I sat there that evening. I felt so fulfilled that Tom was back sitting with me. My white recliner is still in my dining room.

After placing the two older recliners back in their proper place, I told my daughters about it. They couldn't believe what I had done. But my mind was set, and no one could change it!

No one could understand the way I felt unless they'd shared with someone the same joy that Tom and I had shared together in our recliners for years, with all the love we had for each other, even if we were just having a drink or looking at TV or talking about our loving family. I sometimes sit in Tom's recliner, especially to say a prayer.

To this day I thank God that I held on to these recliners to keep me close to Tom and our special memories. He is with me as I watch TV.

Tom and I spending time together in our recliners

EPILOGUE

READING THIS BOOK YOU GET to hear from an extraordinary woman—my grandmother! Her story is one of trials and triumphs but is also a story of truth and love. As the saying goes, "the truth shall set you free". We can only pray that we all will find our truth and purpose to live so boldly in our faith as she has.

It's painful to think about what my life would be or would have been like without my grandmother but I feel it's important to share our thoughts and memories any and every chance we get for the people we love.

Anyone that knows her knows she is indeed "grand" and she has definitely been a "mother" to me through out the years. I'll never forget going to her house every morning for breakfast, the home made Italian lunches she made me for school and her singing in the car on the way there. I can hear her in my head belting it out "Oh Lord in my eyes you were gazing, kindly smiling my name you were saying . . ." Although she sounded a bit nasally she always sings praise loudly and boldly. It puts a smile on my face to think about it.

It has always amazed me how she was able to overcome the odds through her spirituality and connection to God. I feel like we have had many parallels in life and without her I know I wouldn't be the spiritual person that I am today. I was hungry and she fed me, I was naked and she clothed me in the Holy Spirit, I am weak and she showed me the strength. She showed me what it looks like to walk in the spirit.

I know now that it is in our brokenness that we are made whole. Through our loss comes compassion and the kind of love that only a Father can give. There's no question the Holy Spirit moved her to help me and guided her through her own darkness as he showed her the light so she could then be the light for others.

She has overcome so much and has been such a positive influence to many. I have such joyful memories because of my grandmother and the pain comes back to me as I think of what my life would be like without her. She has been saying to me since I was a child "Tu mi chiami no mi scendere"—meaning, you will call my name and I will not come". Although I always get teary eyed and ask her to stop saying that, she always seems peaceful. Where there is perfect love there is no fear and she has only joy of where she is going. When she leaves we will cry because we will feel a great loss but what heaven will gain is a victory, for I believe God rejoices in his children that have been so faithful and true.

The true beauty of this story is in the hope that we can all find joy despite the trials and tribulations that we may go through. And the world can learn from her example and find peace and God in their moments of their storm as I did.

"Grandma I'm so proud of you for sharing your story and inspiring others. Words can never describe our relationship and how much you mean to me. You amaze me—even at 86 it's never too late to write your first book and help others. Your legacy will live on forever in this world and in heaven where you will be reunited with Poppy and Maria. God bless you always and forever! I love you!"

Love,
Joelle xoxoxo

(l-r) Anna Pascale Amodeo, Millie Sadler, Mary Falco Rosamelia

My daughter Kathy Amodeo Ronk and
nephew Anthony Amodeo at their First Holy Communion

The Schaffer Family
Top Row: Amy, (Matthew's wife) my great granddaughter Rebecca,
My grandson Matthew,
Middle Row: My great granddaughters Emily, Morgan and Abigail
Bottom Row: My great granddaughter Katie

My Great Grandaugher Siena Hannaberry.
Daughter of my granddaughter Joelle and Brian Hannaberry.

My Great Grandson Blake Hannaberry.
Son of my granddaughter Joelle and Brian Hannaberry.

CPSIA information can be obtained
at www.ICGtesting.com
Printed in the USA
BVOW03s2134271217
503849BV00001B/31/P